The Economic Benefits of Air Quality Improvements in Arctic Council Countries

OECD

BETTER POLICIES FOR BETTER LIVES

This work is published under the responsibility of the Secretary-General of the OECD. The opinions expressed and arguments employed herein do not necessarily reflect the official views of OECD member countries.

This document, as well as any data and map included herein, are without prejudice to the status of or sovereignty over any territory, to the delimitation of international frontiers and boundaries and to the name of any territory, city or area.

The statistical data for Israel are supplied by and under the responsibility of the relevant Israeli authorities. The use of such data by the OECD is without prejudice to the status of the Golan Heights, East Jerusalem and Israeli settlements in the West Bank under the terms of international law.

Note by Turkey
The information in this document with reference to "Cyprus" relates to the southern part of the Island. There is no single authority representing both Turkish and Greek Cypriot people on the Island. Turkey recognises the Turkish Republic of Northern Cyprus (TRNC). Until a lasting and equitable solution is found within the context of the United Nations, Turkey shall preserve its position concerning the "Cyprus issue".

Note by all the European Union Member States of the OECD and the European Union
The Republic of Cyprus is recognised by all members of the United Nations with the exception of Turkey. The information in this document relates to the area under the effective control of the Government of the Republic of Cyprus.

Please cite this publication as:
OECD (2021), *The Economic Benefits of Air Quality Improvements in Arctic Council Countries*, OECD Publishing, Paris, *https://doi.org/10.1787/9c46037d-en*.

ISBN 978-92-64-71670-4 (print)
ISBN 978-92-64-81327-4 (pdf)

Photo credits: Cover: Village overlooking sea with icebergs © Kedardome - Shutterstock.com.

Corrigenda to publications may be found on line at: *www.oecd.org/about/publishing/corrigenda.htm*.

Foreword

The Arctic is a vital region that helps preserve the balance of the global climate. The Arctic environment is particularly sensitive to short-lived climate pollutants, such as black carbon, which is the most light-absorbing component of particulate matter. Ambitious policy action to reduce air pollution would therefore reduce the negative environmental, health and economic impacts of air pollution, while slowing down climate change by reducing emissions of short-lived climate pollutants.

Due to their proximity to the Arctic region, a central role in reducing air pollution in the Arctic is played by Arctic Council countries, namely Canada, Denmark, Finland, Iceland, Norway, the Russian Federation, Sweden, and the United States. Arctic Council countries have affirmed their support to collectively bring black carbon emissions down by 25-33% by 2025 from 2013 levels. Ambitious policy action to reduce air pollution in Arctic Council countries would help achieve this target.

This report presents a quantitative assessment of the environmental, health and economic consequences of ambitious policy action to reduce air pollution in Arctic Council countries. The scenario analysis is based on a suite of modelling tools to project the impacts of increasingly ambitious policies up to 2050. The report compares a business-as-usual scenario with policy scenarios in which Arctic Council countries, and other regional groupings, adopt the best available techniques to reduce air pollutant emissions, including end-of-pipe technologies, the use of cleaner fuels, and measures to reduce emissions in the agricultural sector.

The modelling shows that these policies could substantially curb emissions of several air pollutants, including bringing black carbon emissions well below the collective target. The benefits would include better air quality, and reductions in air pollution-related premature deaths and illnesses. The costs of achieving the emission reductions would be offset by the economic benefits resulting from improved human and environmental health. When also accounting for the welfare benefits of reduced mortality and pain and suffering from illness, the economic benefits of air pollution policies become substantial.

Overall, the results presented in this report highlight that policy action addressing air pollution in Arctic Council countries could lead to significant environmental, health and welfare benefits, whilst also helping to preserve the Arctic ecosystems.

Rodolfo Lacy, Director, OECD – Environment Directorate

Acknowledgements

This report is an output of the OECD Environmental Policy Committee and its Working Party on Integrating Environmental and Economic Policies (WPIEEP). The report was carried out under the overall responsibility of Shardul Agrawala, Head of the Environment and Economy Integration Division in the OECD Environment Directorate.

This report was written by Elisa Lanzi, Daniel Ostalé Valriberas, Marta Arbinolo, Jean Chateau of the OECD Environment Directorate; Zbigniew Klimont and Chris Heyes of the International Institute for Applied Systems Analysis (IIASA); and Rita Van Dingenen of the European Commission's Joint Research Centre (EC-JRC). The individual inputs of the key contributors are as follows:

OECD	Elisa Lanzi	Project co-ordination and supervision, conceptualisation, projections of economic consequences, drafting, and communication with stakeholders.
	Daniel Ostalé Valriberas	Projections of health impacts and economic consequences, data collection and visualisation and drafting.
	Marta Arbinolo	Conceptualisation, research, data collection and drafting.
	Jean Chateau	Projections of economic consequences, baseline projections.
IIASA	Zbigniew Klimont	Emission scenarios and estimates of costs of emission reductions through deployment of best available techniques.
	Chris Heyes	Emission scenarios, data collection and exchange.
EC-JRC	Rita Van Dingenen	Concentrations, exposure to air pollution, and impacts of air pollution on crop yields.

Ruben Bibas of the OECD Environment Directorate provided support to finalise the projections of economic consequences; Grace Alexander contributed to editing and research; and Katjusha Boffa, Aziza Perrière and Jack McNeill of the OECD Environment Directorate provided administrative support. The report was edited by Fiona Hinchcliffe, and formatted by Annette Hardcastle.

The authors would like to thank Delegates to the Environmental Policy Committee (EPOC) and to the OECD Working Party on Integrating Environmental and Economic Policies (WPIEEP) for useful comments and suggestions on earlier versions of the report. Feedback and comments from Shardul Agrawala, Rob Dellink, and Nils Axel Braathen of the OECD Environment Directorate; Michele Cecchini of the OECD Directorate for Employment, Labour and Social Affairs; Andrés Fuentes Hutfilter and Jolien Noels of the OECD Centre for Entrepreneurship, SMEs & Local Development are all gratefully acknowledged.

The authors also greatly appreciate input and comments from Russel Shearer, co-ordinator of the European Union-funded Action on Black Carbon in the Arctic and Simon Wilson from the Arctic Monitoring and Assessment Programme (AMAP). All scenarios presented in this report were developed with the support of the European Union-funded Action on Black Carbon in the Arctic and the authors gratefully acknowledge the participation in the Action's workshops and the feedback from participants at the workshop.

Finally, this work would not have been possible without the financial support from Finland and Sweden. The views expressed here may not, under any circumstances, be regarded as an official position of the European Commission.

Table of contents

Tables

Figures

Boxes

Acronyms and abbreviations

AC	Arctic Council
AMAP	Arctic Monitoring and Assessment Programme
AMOC	Atlantic Meridional Overturning Circulation
ASEAN	Association of Southeast Asian Nations
BATs	Best available techniques
BC	Black carbon
CGE	Computable general equilibrium
CH_4	Methane
CLE	Current legislation
CLRTAP	Convention on Long-Range Transboundary Air Pollution
CMIP	Coupled Model Intercomparison Project
CO	Carbon monoxide
CO_2	Carbon dioxide
COVID-19	Coronavirus disease 2019
EC-JRC	European Commission's Joint Research Centre
EGBCM	Expert Group on Black Carbon and Methane
EPA	United States Environment Protection Agency
EU	European Union
GAINS	Greenhouse Gas and Air Pollution Interactions and Synergies
GBD	Global Burden of Disease
GDP	Gross domestic product
GHG	Greenhouse gas
IHME	Institute for Health Metrics and Evaluation
IIASA	International Institute for Applied Systems Analysis
IEA	International Energy Agency
IER	Integrated exposure-response
MTFR	Maximum Technically Feasible Reduction
NH_3	Ammonia

NMVOCs	Non-methane volatile organic compounds
NO$_x$	Nitrogen oxides
OC	Organic carbon
OECD	Organisation for Economic Co-operation and Development
O$_3$	Ground-level ozone
PM$_{2.5}$	Fine particulate matter
POPs	Persistent organic pollutants
PPP	Purchasing power parity
SCTP	Standard conditions for temperature and pressure
SDG	Sustainable Development Goals
SDS	Sustainable Development Scenario
SLCP	Short-lived climate pollutant
SO$_2$	Sulphur dioxide
TM5-FASST	Fast Scenario Screening Tool
toe	Tonne(s) of oil equivalent
USD	US dollar
UN	United Nations
VOCs	Volatile organic compounds
VOLY	Value of a life year lost
VSL	Value of a statistical life
WHO	World Health Organization
WTP	Willingness to pay
YOLLs	Years of life lost

Executive summary

The Arctic is a delicate ecosystem that plays a vital role in maintaining stability in the global climate. Changes in the local climate could amplify global warming, with far-reaching consequences for the global environment, human health and well-being.

A range of air pollutants are driving changes in the Arctic region, including greenhouse gases, black carbon – a component of fine particulate matter – and ground-level ozone. These pollutants contribute to atmospheric warming, thus accelerating snow melting and exacerbating the effects of climate change in the Arctic.

Arctic Council countries – Canada, Denmark, Finland, Iceland, Norway, the Russian Federation, Sweden, and the United States – play a central role in reducing air pollution in the Arctic. These countries have affirmed their support to collectively reduce black carbon emissions by 25-33% by 2025 from 2013 levels. In Arctic Council countries, around 18 million people live in areas where fine particle concentrations exceed the World Health Organization (WHO) safe air quality guidelines (10 µg/m^3). Ambitious policy action to reduce emissions of a wide range of air pollutants, including black carbon, would reduce these negative health impacts and contribute to slowing down climate change in the Arctic. But how much would this cost and what would the impacts be on their economies and the health of the region's populations?

This report sets out to answer these questions by providing a quantitative assessment of the biophysical and economic benefits of air pollution policies in Arctic Council countries. The analysis relies on a suite of modelling tools to project the impacts of increasingly ambitious policy action up to 2050, compared with business as usual.

Key findings

- Thanks to policies currently in place and to the deployment of the best available techniques (such as end-of-pipe technologies and the use of cleaner fuels), emissions of air pollutants have been decreasing for some years in Arctic Council countries and are projected to decrease further in the coming decades. Arctic Council countries are projected to come close to meeting the collective black carbon target.

- Additional policies to extensively adopt the best available techniques would allow Arctic Council countries to reduce their emissions more substantially and halve their black carbon emissions by 2025, exceeding their collective target. This would require additional investments in best available techniques especially in the residential and transport sectors.

- These emission reductions would improve air quality and lower populations' exposure to high air pollution levels. In particular, by 2050 the number of people exposed to fine particle concentrations above the WHO air quality guidelines of 10 µg/m^3 would decrease from 18 million to 1 million people. These air quality improvements could avoid four out ten air pollution-related deaths in Arctic Council countries by 2050, as well as thousands of cases of debilitating illnesses, such as chronic bronchitis and childhood asthma.

- These improvements in air quality can be achieved without affecting economic growth. Despite some additional costs for households and firms, this report shows that at the aggregate level, the macroeconomic costs of achieving the emission reductions are offset by the macroeconomic benefits of improved human and environmental health. Such benefits include higher labour productivity, lower health expenditures, and higher agricultural productivity. These aggregate results hide substantial differences across regions. In particular, macroeconomic costs are higher in the Russian Federation, as baseline emissions are higher compared to the other Arctic Council countries.

- Adding the welfare benefits of reduced mortality and pain and suffering from illness, the positive economic consequences of air pollution policies become substantial.

- If other regions of the world also reduced their pollutant emissions, Arctic Council countries would reap additional benefits from lower transboundary air pollution. The competitive position of Arctic Council countries would also improve with widespread international policy action, thus levelling the playing field.

- The implementation of air pollution policies in combination with a sustained energy transition and the achievement of global climate targets would reduce greenhouse gas emissions and air pollutants simultaneously, bringing significant additional health, environmental, and welfare gains.

A call for action

In addition to the many benefits from air pollution policies included in the modelling, there are many others benefits that could not be quantified. These include impacts on biodiversity and ecosystems; preservation of buildings and sites of cultural heritage, and tourism; health effects such as on fertility, cognitive abilities and birth weight. Furthermore, improvements in air quality can also reduce the severity of the respiratory problems caused by viruses such as COVID-19. Taken together, this suggests that the benefits of air pollution policies could be even greater than those quantified in the modelling analysis.

The results presented in this report need to be interpreted bearing in mind the uncertainties surrounding socio-economic projections, emissions estimates, and the biophysical and economic consequences of air pollution policies. However, these uncertainties should not deter policy action. The results clearly highlight that policy action addressing air pollution in Arctic Council countries will lead to significant environmental, health and welfare benefits. In addition, improvements to the local climate in the Arctic can improve the livelihood of local communities, reduce global climate change, and lower the risk of triggering climate tipping points.

1. Air pollution in Arctic Council countries

The fragile Arctic environment is particularly vulnerable to some pollutants that contribute to atmospheric warming, such as black carbon and ground-level ozone. While an important share of air pollutants reach the Arctic from outside the region, emissions from the Arctic Council countries have the greatest impact. This chapter introduces the motivations for policy action on air pollution in Arctic Council countries, highlighting the environmental, health and economic benefits. Particular attention is given to the role of short-lived climate pollutants, and specifically black carbon, whose reduction plays an important role in mitigating climate change. The chapter then provides an overview of the sectoral sources of air pollution in Arctic Council countries.

1.1. Introduction

Air pollution is one of the most serious environmental challenges at the global level, with adverse effects on human health, well-being and the environment. In 2017, outdoor air pollution alone was responsible for approximately 3.5 million deaths (GBD, 2018[1]); in the absence of stricter policies, air pollution-related mortality is projected to reach a global total of 6 to 9 million by 2060 (OECD, 2016[2]). Air pollution also has significant impacts on ecosystems and climate change, as some air pollutants – most notably black carbon and ground-level ozone– are major contributors to atmospheric warming. Such impacts are especially detrimental for fragile environments, such as the Arctic.

Owing to the low population density and limited economic activity characterising the Arctic region, local emissions of air pollutants in the Arctic are limited. An important share of air pollutants reaching the Arctic originates at lower latitudes, highlighting the need to reduce emissions well beyond the Arctic region. Most notably, emissions occurring in Arctic Council (AC) countries have greater impact in the Arctic region, due to their proximity (AMAP, 2015[3]). For this reason, Canada, Denmark, Finland, Iceland, Norway, the Russian Federation (hereafter Russia), Sweden and the United States have affirmed their support to achieve a collective 25-33% reduction of black carbon emissions by 2025 compared to 2013 levels (Arctic Council, 2019[4]).

Alongside concerns about black carbon emissions, Arctic Council countries have put in place policies to reduce emissions of a wide range of air pollutants. Besides delivering environmental and health benefits, improved air quality can have positive effects on the economy, increasing labour productivity and crop yields while lowering health expenditures (OECD, 2016[2]). Recent literature has focused on the economic benefits of improved air quality and on the additional co-benefits of climate policies (Amann et al., 2020[5]; Harmsen et al., 2020[6]; Markandya et al., 2018[7]; Amann et al., 2017[8]; Vandyck et al., 2018[9]). For example, Vandyck et al. (2018[9]) demonstrate that the air quality co-benefits of climate policy alone counterbalance the costs of meeting the Nationally Determined Contributions that countries presented under the Paris Agreement. Recent evidence from the empirical literature also highlights the substantial economic benefits of reducing air pollution (Dechezleprêtre, Rivers and Stadler, 2019[10]).

This report contributes to the existing literature by quantifying the economic consequences of implementing policies that directly target air pollution in Arctic Council countries. In particular, the report compares the outcomes of five scenarios:

- A baseline scenario that assumes the continuation of air pollution policies and legislation already in place.
- A scenario in which Arctic Council countries implement additional policies to reduce air pollution.
- A scenario in which these policies are also implemented in the 13 Observer countries to the Arctic Council.[1]
- A scenario that assumes the global implementation of these policies.
- An integrated policy scenario, in which these air pollution policies are implemented alongside ambitious climate and energy transition policies.[2]

While this analysis focuses primarily on the benefits of policy action in Arctic Council countries by comparing current legislation with additional policy action in these countries, the additional scenarios consider two important aspects that can influence the success of air pollution policies: transboundary air pollution, and integrated policy action across different environmental domains. In all policy scenarios, air pollutant emissions are reduced through policy-induced adoption of the best available techniques (BATs). Such policies target a wide range of air pollutants, aiming to improve air quality. Specifically, this report considers emissions of black carbon (BC), organic carbon (OC), sulphur dioxide (SO_2), nitrogen oxides (NO_x), non-methane volatile organic compounds (NMVOCs), nitrous oxide (N_2O), carbon monoxide (CO), and ammonia (NH_3).[3] These pollutants are particularly relevant as they drive the concentrations of fine particulate matter ($PM_{2.5}$) and ground-level ozone (O_3).

Building on the report *The Economic Consequences of Outdoor Air Pollution* (OECD, 2016[2]), this report adopts a modelling approach that links economic activity to projected emissions, pollutant concentrations, the biophysical impacts of outdoor air pollution, and their feedback effects on the economy. The main modelling tool used in the analysis is the OECD ENV-Linkages model (Chateau, Dellink and Lanzi, 2014[11]), which can quantify the economic consequences of air pollution to 2050. This economic analysis is supported by results from the Greenhouse Gas and Air Pollution Interactions and Synergies (GAINS) model developed by the International Institute for Applied Systems Analysis (IIASA),[4] which provides projections of air pollutant emissions, as well as the costs of adopting BATs to reduce air pollution (Amann et al., 2011[12]; Höglund-Isaksson et al., 2020[13]; Winiwarter et al., 2018[14]; Klimont et al., 2017[15]). Finally, the TM5-FASST model developed by the Joint Research Centre of the European Commission links emission projections with human exposure to $PM_{2.5}$ and ground-level ozone pollution (Van Dingenen et al., 2018[16]).

The economic consequences of air pollution policies are quantified in this report by considering two complementary aspects: (1) macroeconomic effects; and (2) welfare improvements. The macroeconomic effects result from the market impacts of air pollution, which affect specific sectors resulting in changes in economic growth and gross domestic product (GDP). Welfare improvements account for the impacts of air pollution on well-being and, in this report, they result from changes in the incidence of air pollution-related mortality and illness. The macroeconomic effects are calculated in ENV-Linkages considering both the benefits and associated costs of reducing emissions and improving air quality. Drawing on previous OECD analysis (OECD, 2016[2]), the benefits are calculated estimating the improvements in labour productivity and agricultural productivity and the decrease in health expenditures that would result from improved air quality. The emission reduction costs are included in ENV-Linkages as additional sector-specific costs for firms and households, based on the costs the BATs from the GAINS model. Meanwhile, welfare improvements from air pollution policies are quantified using valuation techniques that attribute a monetary value to lives lost and to the pain and suffering associated with illness.

This report is structured as follows. The rest of Chapter 1 highlights the main motivations for policy action to reduce air pollution in Arctic Council countries and provides an overview of the sources, distribution and impacts of air pollution in these countries. Chapter 2 outlines the methodology used for the modelling analysis and describes the policy scenarios studied in the report. Chapter 3 presents the emission and concentration projections as well as the health benefits from policy action on air pollution. Chapter 4 outlines the economic consequences of the policy scenarios, including both macroeconomic and welfare effects. Chapter 5 illustrates possible additional benefits from wider geographical adoption of air pollution policies and from integrated air pollution, climate and energy transition policies. Finally, Chapter 6 discusses the overall benefits of air pollution policies, also consdiering the additional benefits of policy action that could not be included in the modelling analysis, and concludes with a call for action on air pollution.

1.2. The focus of Arctic Council countries on air pollution

Air pollution is one of the most serious environmental challenges of our times, due to its severe effects on human health and the environment. The impacts of air pollution – and in particular of short-lived climate pollutants (SLCPs) – are particularly detrimental for the fragile Arctic environment due to the region's exceptional sensitivity to local and global temperature changes (EPA, 2012[17]). SLCPs are air pollutants that also have a warming impact on the climate. They include black carbon (Box 1.1), methane, ground-level ozone, and hydrofluorocarbons.[5]

While local emissions contribute significantly to air pollution in the Arctic region, most pollutants affecting the Arctic are transported to the region from lower latitudes by the wind (AMAP, 2015[3]). As a consequence, emission reductions occurring in the whole territory of the eight Arctic Council countries can largely help to preserve air quality in the Arctic. Emission reductions in other regions – and particularly in the 13 Observer countries to the Arctic Council (Table 1.1) – can contribute further to reducing pollutant concentrations in the Arctic.

Table 1.1. Arctic Council countries and Observers

Arctic Council countries	Arctic Council Observers	
Canada	France	India
United States	Germany	Korea
Russian Federation	Italy	Singapore
Denmark	Japan	Spain
Finland	Netherlands	Switzerland
Iceland	People's Republic of China (hereafter, China)	United Kingdom
Norway	Poland	
Sweden		

Source: (Arctic Council, 2021[18]).

In recent years, Arctic Council countries have increased their engagement for addressing air pollution. Owing to its effect on the local and global climate (Box 1.1), black carbon has become a major concern for these countries, which have set an aspirational collective target to reduce their aggregate BC emissions from between 25 to 33% by 2025 compared to 2013 levels (Arctic Council, 2019[4]).[6]

Besides helping to preserve the Arctic environment, improved air quality in the region would also have economic and health benefits throughout the whole territory of the eight Arctic Council countries. These benefits would be particularly significant in densely populated areas characterised by high levels of economic activity, as well as in agricultural areas. Indeed, lower pollution levels lead to improved health and improved agricultural productivity (Van Dingenen et al., 2009[19]; Holland, 2014[20]; OECD, 2016[2]).

The health impacts of outdoor air pollution in Arctic Council countries are large. The Global Burden of Disease (GBD) project estimates that in 2017, over 420 000 people died from air pollution in the region, accounting for almost 9% of all deaths in Arctic Council countries that year (GBD, 2018[21]). In addition, human exposure to high concentrations of $PM_{2.5}$ increases the risk of cardiovascular diseases (e.g. cardiac arrhythmia, stroke, and coronary and ischaemic heart disease), respiratory problems (e.g. asthma, bronchitis, and pulmonary dysfunctions), lung cancer, respiratory infections, diabetes and kidney failure. Furthermore, exposure to $PM_{2.5}$ is associated with adverse birth and nervous system outcomes, reduced cognitive functions and accelerated biological aging. Exposure to ground-level ozone is also responsible for respiratory diseases, leading to significant levels of mortality and morbidity. Lower concentrations of fine particulate matter and ground-level ozone would reduce the incidence of air pollution-related illnesses and deaths (GBD, 2018[21]).

Box 1.1. Black carbon and climate change in the Arctic

Black carbon is a primary component of fine particulate matter and can have serious impacts on human health and the environment. Although the eight Arctic Council countries are responsible for 8% of black carbon emissions globally, they are responsible for 30% of BC's warming effect in the Arctic (AMAP, 2015[3]).

Due to its dark colour, BC is the most light-absorbing component of particulate matter and, as such, it is a major contributor to climate change. BC is a short-lived climate pollutant with a strong atmospheric warming potential. It is the second-largest anthropogenic contributor to global warming after carbon dioxide (CO_2) (Yang et al., 2019[22]; Bond et al., 2013[23]; Shrestha, Traina and Swanston, 2010[24]; Moffet and Prather, 2009[25]; AMAP, 2019[26]). Despite its short lifetime in the air, the radiative forcing of one gram of black carbon is comparable to that of a ton of carbon dioxide (CCAC and WHO, 2015[27]).

Besides sparking a warming effect when suspended in the atmosphere, black carbon further interferes with the Arctic climate when it is deposited on snow and ice cover, darkening the surface and thus decreasing the albedo, i.e. the ability to reflect solar radiation (AMAP, 2015[3]). The Arctic region is particularly vulnerable to the effects of BC deposition, due to the presence of large snow and ice-covered surfaces. The dark coat accelerates ice and snow melting while warming the atmosphere (AMAP, 2015[3]). In recent decades, BC deposition alone has accounted for 0.5 to 1°C of warming in the Arctic (Bice et al., 2009[28]). A recent study of Greenlandic snow cover suggests that snow albedo might decrease by over 10% by the end of the century (Tedesco et al., 2016[29]).

Nonetheless, black carbon is co-emitted and can interact with other pollutants, some of which – such as sulphur dioxide (SO_2) – can have a counterbalancing cooling effect (AMAP, 2015[3]; Smith et al., 2020[30]). In some instances, black carbon itself can lead to a slight cooling effect, as BC particles facilitate cloud condensation, thus enhancing cloud reflectivity. Since BC emissions are always accompanied by cooling effects, climate modelling studies have shown that the climate mitigation potential of BC is relatively small and highly uncertain (Kühn et al., 2020[31]).

Despite these uncertainties, the possible impacts of black carbon on the Arctic climate represent a major threat in and beyond the Arctic region. Arctic warming accelerates sea level rise and interferes with the water cycle, increasing the risk of floods and droughts and affecting water availability in other regions of the world. For this reason, and given the multifaceted effects of black carbon pollution, policies targeting BC have the advantage of addressing the challenge of climate change and air pollution simultaneously.

Besides affecting human health, air pollution also has adverse effects on plant development and health. Ground-level ozone is absorbed by leaves, where it induces cell death and reduces physiological functions. Thus, high concentrations of ground-level ozone lead to slower growth, reduced flowering and lower seed production, hindering crop yield and quality (Latha et al., 2017[32]).

As a consequence, the biophysical impacts of outdoor air pollution entail substantial economic costs (OECD, 2016[2]; OECD, 2014[33]; Roy and Braathen, 2017[34]), which result from (1) losses in labour productivity; (2) additional health expenditures; (3) lower agricultural productivity; and (4) the welfare costs of air pollution-related mortality and suffering as a result of illness.

1.3. Anthropogenic sources of air pollution in Arctic Council countries

In the Arctic Council region, the largest contributors to the emission of black carbon and organic carbon – both components of primary PM2.5 – are the energy and industrial sectors, together with residential wood burning, and transport.[7] While Arctic Council countries have set an aspirational emission reduction target for black carbon, substantial health benefits can only be achieved if other pollutants are also reduced. Specifically, reducing emissions of total primary $PM_{2.5}$ and of other air pollutants that contribute to the formation of secondary $PM_{2.5}$ is necessary to reduce $PM_{2.5}$ pollution, which is the main driver of the health impacts of air pollution (Box 1.2). Abating emissions of gases which form secondary $PM_{2.5}$ (precursor gases), such as sulphur dioxide, nitrogen oxides, ammonia, and non-methane volatile organic compounds, could further contribute to reducing the concentration of fine particles in the atmosphere.

Box 1.2. What are primary and secondary pollutants?

Pollutants can be classified into primary and secondary pollutants depending on how they are generated. Primary pollutants, such as carbon monoxide and sulphur dioxide, are the direct by-product of human activities. Secondary pollutants, such as ground-level ozone, are formed when primary (or precursor) pollutants react with other elements in the atmosphere. Some pollutants, such as NO_X and NMVOCs, are precursor gases of both ground-level ozone and $PM_{2.5}$.

$PM_{2.5}$ is both a primary and secondary pollutant. Therefore, both primary and secondary $PM_{2.5}$ are taken into account in air pollution measurements. Primary $PM_{2.5}$ is emitted directly into the atmosphere by activities such as the combustion of fossil fuels and road transport. Particles composing primary $PM_{2.5}$ include organic carbon and black carbon. Secondary $PM_{2.5}$ is generated when $PM_{2.5}$ precursors such as sulphur dioxide, nitrogen oxides, volatile organic compounds and ammonia react with other elements in the atmosphere. This process can take place far away from the original emission source (Hodan and Barnard, 2004[35]).

Ground-level ozone is a secondary pollutant, as it is not directly emitted into the atmosphere. Ground-level ozone is an example of photochemical oxidants, i.e. it is formed from the interaction between sunlight and precursor gases – mainly volatile organic compounds, nitrogen oxides, carbon monoxide and methane (CH_4) (Unger et al., 2006[36]).

Meteorological and climatic conditions, such as atmospheric temperature, play a role in the chemical interactions occurring in the atmosphere (Lam et al., 2011[37]). For example, a rise in global temperatures could result in higher concentrations of ground-level ozone and secondary $PM_{2.5}$. Other climatic factors, such as the frequency of precipitation and the presence of sunlight, can also influence the formation of secondary pollutants. For instance, the higher levels of sunlight in the summer months facilitate the formation of ground-level ozone.

Transport is an important source of air pollution in Arctic Council countries. It contributes significantly to the formation of $PM_{2.5}$ and ground-level ozone. According to estimates of IIASA's GAINS model, in 2015 transport accounts for around 70% of CO emissions, half[8] of NO_X and BC emissions and for one-quarter of OC and NMVOCs emissions in the region (Figure 1.1).

The industry and energy sectors are other key sources of pollution in Arctic Council countries. Together, energy production and consumption and the industrial sector are responsible for nearly all SO_2 emissions and one-third of NMVOCs and NO_X emissions in the region. These sectors are also responsible for a significant share of BC (18%) and OC (6%) emissions (Figure 1.1). Flaring[9] alone represents 7% of total anthropogenic NMVOCs and 14% of black carbon emissions.

The residential sector is a key contributor to the formation of primary and secondary $PM_{2.5}$ and ground-level ozone. In particular, the combustion of solid and liquid fuels for domestic heating is a major source of organic carbon (40%) and black carbon (over 20%), while also contributing to NMVOCs (10%), NO_X (5%) and SO_2 (3%) emissions in the region (Figure 1.1).

Finally, the agricultural sector is a major contributor of NH_3 (92%), and it also has an important role in the emission of NMVOCs (27%) and OC (20%) (Figure 1.1). Agricultural fires,[10] which are often used to dispose of crop residues, are responsible for nearly all the OC, NMVOCs and BC emissions from the sector and for 70% of primary $PM_{2.5}$ emissions in the region.

Figure 1.1. Emissions of air pollutants in Arctic Council countries

Sectoral shares in 2015

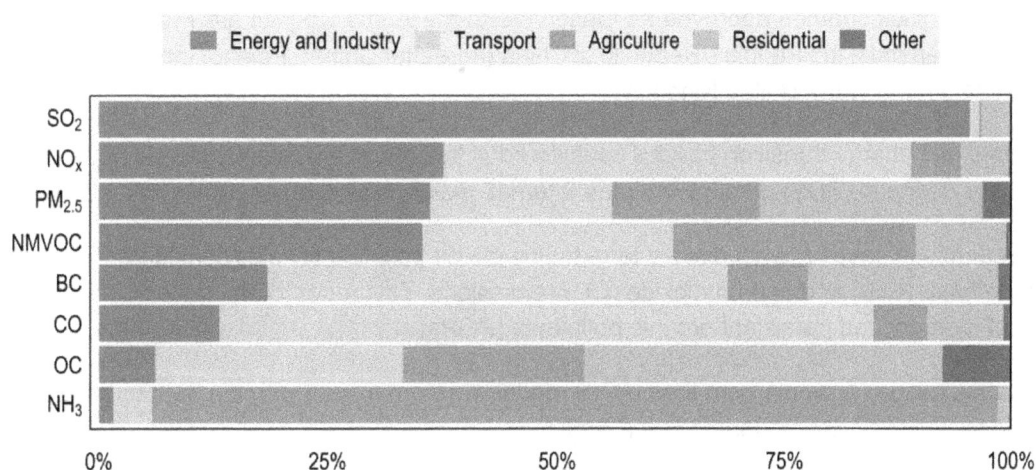

Note: "Residential" emissions are due to wood and fuel burning. "Other" includes emissions from the waste sector (except agricultural waste, which is included in "Agriculture"). In this figure, $PM_{2.5}$ refers to primary emissions only.
Source: IIASA's GAINS model.

StatLink ᵐˢ🔒 https://stat.link/p6m9lr

Although ground-level ozone is not directly emitted to the atmosphere, human activities contribute to the emission of its precursor gases, which include methane, NMVOCs, NO_x, and CO. In Arctic Council countries, the transport, industry and power generation sectors emit large shares of these pollutants (Figure 1.1). Most notably, emissions of methane and CO, which are particularly relevant to ground-level ozone formation, are largely driven by industry and energy-related emissions and by transport emissions.

Other emission sources in the Arctic Council region – such as shipping and gas and oil flaring – are only included as part of aggregate emissions of Arctic Council countries, as their projections are characterised by high levels of uncertainty that did not allow emissions to be distinguished by country. Shipping activities in the Arctic are projected to keep growing, potentially quadrupling by 2050 (AMAP, 2015[3]) as reduced ice cover will open new shipping routes and opportunities across the region's seas. However, navigating in Arctic waters implies significant costs, which might reduce the net economic gains of shorter transit routes (ITF, 2019[38]), thus making the sector's development in the region rather uncertain. Emissions from flaring activities are also subject to uncertainty due to the variation in gas and oil composition and in flaring operating practices (Huang and Fu, 2016[39]; Conrad and Johnson, 2017[40]; Conrad and Johnson, 2017[40]; Klimont et al., 2017[15]; Stohl et al., 2013[41]).[11] Flaring inventories and projections are particularly uncertain for key emitters, such as Russia, due to the lack of detailed activity data for a wide array of sources, and of a country-specific emission factor[12] (Böttcher et al., forthcoming[42]).

Finally, emissions from wildfires – which are also highly uncertain – are not included in the emission projections presented in this report, although they are accounted for in the calculations of pollutant concentrations (Section 3.2). Wildfires are an important and increasing source of several pollutants (van Marle et al., 2017[43]) that also contribute to global warming, including black carbon. In Europe and North

America, the frequency of wildfires has increased in recent years, and wildfire locations have changed too, moving towards more northern latitudes. Climate change is estimated to have a considerable impact on this trend. Indeed, increasing temperatures and changes in precipitation patterns leading to arid conditions and lower soil moisture facilitate the development and spread of forest fires (Arctic Council, 2019[4]).

Notes

[1] The 13 non-Arctic countries approved as Observers to the Arctic Council are France, Germany, Italy, Japan, the Netherlands, the People's Republic of China (hereafter China), Poland, India, Korea, Singapore, Spain, Switzerland, and the United Kingdom.

[2] The climate and energy transition policies considered in this report are those included in the Sustainable Development Scenario (SDS) presented by the International Energy Agency (IEA) (IEA, 2018[46]).

[3] While greenhouse gases are not directly targeted by the air pollution policies considered, this report also looks at methane (CH_4) and carbon dioxide (CO_2) emissions. This report does not include the long-range transport of mercury and persistent organic pollutants (POPs).

[4] All scenarios based on inputs from the GAINS model were developed with the support of the European Union-funded Action on Black Carbon in the Arctic.

[5] Chapter 6 in this report also discusses the specific impacts of SLCP emissions in more detail.

[6] For simplicity, the report will refer to policy action to reduce black carbon as the collective target.

[7] Regional estimates of pollutant emissions by sector are obtained using the GAINS model developed by IIASA (Rao et al., 2016[44]; Amann, Klimont and Wagner, 2013[45]; Amann et al., 2011[12]). All emission figures in this Chapter refer to 2015.

[8] All the emission rates presented in this chapter refer to Arctic Council countries' totals, unless otherwise specified.

[9] Gas flaring is a combustion process that burns associated, unwanted or excess gases and liquids released during many industrial processes, such as oil and gas extraction or refineries.

[10] Other types of fires, such as forest and grassland fires, represent major sources of air pollution but are not linked to the agricultural sector.

[11] Gas and oil composition can vary substantially across different oil and gas fields, and is also severely affected by environmental conditions such as temperature and atmospheric pressure.

[12] Country-specific emission factors allow to activity levels to be linked to emission levels at the national scale, rather than relying on regional or global averages.

References

Amann, M. et al. (2011), "Cost-effective control of air quality and greenhouse gases in Europe: Modeling and policy applications", *Environmental Modelling & Software*, Vol. 26/12, pp. 1489-1501, http://dx.doi.org/10.1016/j.envsoft.2011.07.012. [12]

Amann, M. et al. (2017), *Costs, Benefits and Economic Impacts of the EU Clean Air Strategy and their Implications on Innovation and Competitiveness*, International Institute for Applied Systems Analysis (IIASA). [8]

Amann, M. et al. (2020), "Reducing global air pollution: the scope for further policy interventions", *Philosophical Transactions of the Royal Society A: Mathematical, Physical and Engineering Sciences*, Vol. 378/2183, p. 20190331, http://dx.doi.org/10.1098/rsta.2019.0331. [5]

Amann, M., Z. Klimont and F. Wagner (2013), "Regional and global emissions of air pollutants: recent trends and future scenarios", *Annual Review of Environment and Resources*, Vol. 38/1, pp. 31-55, http://dx.doi.org/10.1146/annurev-environ-052912-173303. [45]

AMAP (2019), *Review of Reporting Systems for National Black Carbon Emissions Inventories*, AMAP, Tromsø, https://www.amap.no/documents/doc/eua-bca-technical-report-2/1780 (accessed on 16 December 2019). [26]

AMAP (2015), *Summary for Policy-makers: Arctic Climate Issues 2015*, AMAP, Tromsø, https://www.amap.no/documents/doc/summary-for-policy-makers-arctic-climate-issues-2015/1196 (accessed on 4 December 2020). [3]

Arctic Council (2021), *Arctic Council - Observers*, https://arctic-council.org/en/about/observers/ (accessed on 10 March 2021). [18]

Arctic Council (2019), *Expert Group on Black Carbon and Methane - Summary of Progress and Reccomendations*, https://oaarchive.arctic-council.org/handle/11374/2411 (accessed on 9 March 2021). [4]

Bice, K. et al. (2009), *Black Carbon: A Review and Policy Recommendations*, Princeton University, https://www.princeton.edu/~mauzeral/WWS591e/Princeton.WWS591E.Black.Carbon.report.2009.pdf. [28]

Bond, T. et al. (2013), "Bounding the Role of Black Carbon in the Climate System: A Scientific Assessment", *Journal of Geophysical Research Atmospheres*, Vol. 118/11, pp. 5380-5552, http://dx.doi.org/10.1002/jgrd.50171. [23]

Böttcher, K. et al. (forthcoming), "Black carbon emissions from flaring in Russia in the period 2012-2017". [42]

CCAC and WHO (2015), *Reducing Global Health Risks Through Mitigation of Short-lived Climate Pollutants: Scoping report for policymakers*, World Health Organization, Geneva, https://www.who.int/phe/publications/climate-reducing-health-risks/en/. [27]

Chateau, J., R. Dellink and E. Lanzi (2014), "An Overview of the OECD ENV-Linkages Model: Version 3", *OECD Environment Working Papers*, No. 65, OECD Publishing, Paris, https://dx.doi.org/10.1787/5jz2qck2b2vd-en. [11]

Conrad, B. and M. Johnson (2017), "Field Measurements of Black Carbon Yields from Gas Flaring", *Environmental Science & Technology*, Vol. 51/3, pp. 1893-1900, http://dx.doi.org/10.1021/acs.est.6b03690. [40]

Dechezleprêtre, A., N. Rivers and B. Stadler (2019), "The economic cost of air pollution: Evidence from Europe"*, OECD Economics Department Working Papers*, No. 1584, OECD Publishing, Paris, https://dx.doi.org/10.1787/56119490-en. [10]

EPA (2012), *Report to Congress on Black Carbon*, United States Environmental Protection Agency, https://www3.epa.gov/airquality/blackcarbon/2012report/fullreport.pdf. [17]

GBD (2018), *Global Burden of Disease Study 2017 (GBD 2017) Burden by Risk 1990-2017, Global Burden of Disease Collaborative Network.*, Seattle, United States: Institute for Health Metrics and Evaluation (IHME), http://ghdx.healthdata.org/record/ihme-data/gbd-2017-burden-risk-1990-2017 (accessed on 25 March 2021). [1]

GBD (2018), "Global Burden of Disease Study 2017: All cause Mortality and Life Expectancy 1950-2017, Global Burden of Disease Collaborative Network.", *Seattle, United States: Institute for Health Metrics and Evaluation (IHME)*. [21]

Harmsen, M. et al. (2020), "Co-benefits of black carbon mitigation for climate and air quality", *Climatic Change*, http://dx.doi.org/10.1007/s10584-020-02800-8. [6]

Hodan, W. and W. Barnard (2004), "Evaluating the Contribution of PM2.5 Precursor Gases and Re-entrained Road Emissions to Mobile Source PM2.5 Particulate Matter Emissions Prepared by MACTEC Under Contract to the Federal Highway Administration", *MACTEC Federal Programs, Research Triangle Park, NC.*. [35]

Höglund-Isaksson, L. et al. (2020), "Technical potentials and costs for reducing global anthropogenic methane emissions in the 2050 timeframe −results from the GAINS model", *Environmental Research Communications*, Vol. 2/2, p. 025004, http://dx.doi.org/10.1088/2515-7620/ab7457. [13]

Holland, M. (2014), *Cost-benefit Analysis of Final Policy Scenarios for the EU Clean Air Package*, http://ec.europa.eu/environment/air/pdf/TSAP%20CBA.pdf (accessed on 10 January 2018). [20]

Huang, K. and J. Fu (2016), "A Global Gas Flaring Black Carbon Emission Rate Dataset from 1994 to 2012", *Scientific Data*, http://dx.doi.org/10.1038/sdata.2016.104. [39]

IEA (2018), *World Energy Outlook 2018*, International Energy Agency, Paris, https://dx.doi.org/10.1787/weo-2018-en. [46]

ITF (2019), *ITF Transport Outlook 2019*, OECD Publishing, Paris, https://dx.doi.org/10.1787/transp_outlook-en-2019-en. [38]

Klimont, Z. et al. (2017), "Global Anthropogenic Emissions of Particulate Matter Including Black Carbon", *Atmospheric Chemistry and Physics*, Vol. 17/14, pp. 8681-8723, http://dx.doi.org/10.5194/acp-17-8681-2017. [15]

Kühn, T. et al. (2020), "Effects of black carbon mitigation on Arctic climate", *Atmospheric Chemistry and Physics*, Vol. 20/9, pp. 5527-5546, http://dx.doi.org/10.5194/acp-20-5527-2020. [31]

Lam, Y. et al. (2011), "Impacts of future climate change and effects of biogenic emissions on surface ozone and particulate matter concentrations in the United States", *Atmospheric Chemistry and Physics*, Vol. 11/10, pp. 4789-4806, http://dx.doi.org/10.5194/acp-11-4789-2011. [37]

Latha, R. et al. (2017), "Absorbing Aerosols, Possible Implication to Crop Yield - A Comparison between IGB Stations", *Aerosol and Air Quality Research*, Vol. 17/3, pp. 693-705, http://dx.doi.org/10.4209/aaqr.2016.02.0054. [32]

Markandya, A. et al. (2018), "Health Co-benefits from Air Pollution and Mitigation Costs of the Paris Agreement: A Modelling Study", *Lancet Planet Health*, Vol. 2, pp. 126-33, https://doi.org/10.1016/S2542-5196(18)30029-9. [7]

Moffet, R. and K. Prather (2009), "In-situ Measurements of the Mixing State and Optical Properties of Soot with Implications for Radiative Forcing Estimates", *Proceedings of the National Academy of Sciences of the United States of America*, Vol. 106/29, pp. 11872-11877, http://dx.doi.org/10.1073/pnas.0900040106. [25]

OECD (2016), *The Economic Consequences of Outdoor Air Pollution*, OECD Publishing, Paris, https://dx.doi.org/10.1787/9789264257474-en. [2]

OECD (2014), *The Cost of Air Pollution: Health Impacts of Road Transport*, OECD Publishing, Paris, https://dx.doi.org/10.1787/9789264210448-en. [33]

Rao, S. et al. (2016), "A multi-model assessment of the co-benefits of climate mitigation for global air quality", *Environmental Research Letters*, Vol. 11/12, p. 124013, http://dx.doi.org/10.1088/1748-9326/11/12/124013. [44]

Roy, R. and N. Braathen (2017), "The Rising Cost of Ambient Air Pollution Thus Far in the 21st Century: Results from the BRIICS and the OECD Countries", *OECD Environment Working Papers*, No. 124, OECD Publishing, Paris, https://doi.org/10.1787/19970900 (accessed on 26 April 2019). [34]

Shrestha, G., S. Traina and C. Swanston (2010), "Black Carbon's Properties and Role in the Environment: A Comprehensive Review", *Sustainability*, Vol. 2, pp. 294-320, http://dx.doi.org/10.3390/su2010294. [24]

Smith, S. et al. (2020), "Impact of methane and black carbon mitigation on forcing and temperature: a multi-model scenario analysis", *Climatic Change*, http://dx.doi.org/10.1007/s10584-020-02794-3. [30]

Stohl, A. et al. (2013), "Black carbon in the Arctic: the underestimated role of gas flaring and residential combustion emissions", *Atmospheric Chemistry and Physics*, Vol. 13/17, pp. 8833-8855, http://dx.doi.org/10.5194/acp-13-8833-2013. [41]

Tedesco, M. et al. (2016), "The darkening of the Greenland ice sheet: trends, drivers, and projections (1981–2100)", *The Cryosphere*, Vol. 10/2, pp. 477-496, http://dx.doi.org/10.5194/tc-10-477-2016. [29]

Unger, N. et al. (2006), "Cross influences of ozone and sulfate precursor emissions changes on air quality and climate", *Proceedings of the National Academy of Sciences of the United States of America*, Vol. 103/12, pp. 4377-4380, http://dx.doi.org/10.1073/pnas.0508769103. [36]

Van Dingenen, R. et al. (2018), "TM5-FASST: A Global Atmospheric Source–receptor Model for Rapid Impact Analysis of Emission Changes on Air Quality and Short-lived Climate Pollutants", *Atmospheric Chemistry and Physics*, Vol. 18, pp. 16173-16211, https://doi.org/10.5194/acp-18-16173-2018. [16]

Van Dingenen, R. et al. (2009), "The global impact of ozone on agricultural crop yields under current and future air quality legislation", *Atmospheric Environment*, Vol. 43/3, pp. 604-618, http://dx.doi.org/10.1016/j.atmosenv.2008.10.033. [19]

van Marle, M. et al. (2017), "Historic global biomass burning emissions for CMIP6 (BB4CMIP) based on merging satellite observations with proxies and fire models (1750–2015)", *Geoscientific Model Development*, Vol. 10/9, pp. 3329-3357, http://dx.doi.org/10.5194/gmd-10-3329-2017. [43]

Vandyck, T. et al. (2018), "Air quality co-benefits for human health and agriculture counterbalance costs to meet Paris Agreement pledges", *Nature Communications*, Vol. 9/1, http://dx.doi.org/10.1038/s41467-018-06885-9. [9]

Winiwarter, W. et al. (2018), "Technical opportunities to reduce global anthropogenic emissions of nitrous oxide", *Environmental Research Letters*, Vol. 13/1, p. 014011, http://dx.doi.org/10.1088/1748-9326/aa9ec9. [14]

Yang, Y. et al. (2019), "Variability, Timescales, and Nonlinearity in Climate Responses to Black Carbon Emissions", *Atmospheric Chemistry and Physics*, Vol. 19/4, pp. 2405-2420, http://dx.doi.org/10.5194/acp-19-2405-2019. [22]

2. Description of the approach and scenarios

The methodology used to analyse the economic consequences of policies targeting air quality in Arctic Council countries is described in this chapter. This methodology requires multiple steps, from creating plausible economic projections and changes in air pollutant emissions, to calculating concentrations of key pollutants, the biophysical impacts on health and crop yields, and the economic consequences of the policy scenarios. The scenario analysis relies on the OECD ENV-Linkages model, along with IIASA's GAINS model and the European Commission JRC's TM5-FASST model.

2.1. Scenarios overview

This report analyses the economic consequences of policies targeting air pollution, based on a scenario analysis performed with the OECD Computable General Equilibrium (CGE) model ENV-Linkages (Chateau, Dellink and Lanzi, 2014[1]). The report compares four policy scenarios to a reference baseline scenario, all with a 2050 time horizon (Table 2.1; see also Chapter 1).

Table 2.1. Overview and regional coverage of scenarios

Scenario label	Scenario description	Arctic Council countries	Observer countries	Rest of the world
CLE	Current Legislation (Baseline)	CLE	CLE	CLE
MTFR-AC	Maximum Technically Feasible Reduction in Arctic Council countries only	MTFR	CLE	CLE
MTFR-AC&Obs	Maximum Technically Feasible Reduction in Arctic Council and Observer countries	MTFR	MTFR	CLE
MTFR-Global	Maximum Technically Feasible Reduction at the global level	MTFR	MTFR	MTFR
MTFR-SDS	Maximum Technically Feasible Reduction and Sustainable Development Scenario at the global level	MTFR - SDS	MTFR – SDS	MTFR - SDS

The baseline scenario assumes the effective implementation of the **current legislation (CLE)** in the eight Arctic Council countries. The legislation considered addresses air pollution from combustion plants, industrial processes, road and non-road vehicles, shipping, agriculture, and use of solvents and paint, as well as residential emissions.

The CLE scenario is compared with four policy action scenarios that reflect the implementation of **maximum technically feasible reductions (MTFR)** to abate pollutant emissions. The MTFR scenario explores the extent to which emissions could be further reduced through the policy-induced application of all existing best available techniques (BATs), in addition to the implementation of current regulations.

The main policy scenario analysed in this report considers the achievement of the maximum technically-feasible emission reductions in the eight Arctic Council countries, referred to as the **MTFR-AC** scenario. For this scenario, data on the investments needed to reduce air pollution are provided by the GAINS model and included in ENV-Linkages (see Section 2.2) below on the modelling framework).

As emission reductions in other regions can also contribute to improving air quality in Arctic Council countries through reduced transboundary air pollution, two additional scenarios are considered: one in which MTFR technologies are also adopted in Arctic Council Observer countries (referred to as **MTFR-AC&Obs**), and one representing the global deployment of the MTFR technologies (**MTFR-Global**).

Finally, an additional scenario (**MTFR-SDS**) considers integrated policy action across different environmental domains, focusing on the interaction among air pollution, climate and energy transition policies. This scenario assumes that the policies of the **MTFR-Global** scenario are complemented by the climate and energy policies.

All scenarios are are designed based on inputs from the Greenhouse Gas and Air Pollution Interactions and Synergies (GAINS) model developed by the International Institute for Applied Systems Analysis (IIASA) (Box 2.1). The MTFR-SDS scenario reflects the climate and energy policies included in the

International Energy Agency (IEA)'s Sustainable Development Scenario (SDS) presented in the 2018 World Energy Outlook (IEA, 2018[2]) (Box 2.2).

While a full analysis of the costs and benefits of the deployment of MTFR technologies is only presented for the MTFR-AC scenario, the three additional scenarios highlight the importance of wider policy action in the fight against air pollution. For these scenarios, only the welfare improvements are presented, as a full assessment of the macroeconomic consequences of these scenarios is beyond the scope of this report.

Box 2.1. The GAINS model's emission abatement scenarios

The scenarios analysed in this report are based on inputs from IIASA's GAINS integrated assessment model, which provides projections of air pollutants, emission reduction potentials, as well as the cost of emission reductions (Amann et al., 2011[3]; Höglund-Isaksson et al., 2020[4]; Winiwarter et al., 2018[5]; Klimont et al., 2017[6]). The emission projections provided by the GAINS model stem from projections of economic activities, and rely on specific assumptions about current environmental legislations as well as existing technical options to reduce air pollution. While GAINS offers a coherent framework to assess emission projections, its projections can differ from the ones developed by individual countries. Data quality varies across countries and, for those cases in which information is missing, the model's default assumptions are applied. These include representative emission factors, which reflect the state of technology deployment in a country, assumptions about the shares of specific technologies to achieve a given emission standard, and sometimes also alternative sources of activity data (e.g. peer reviewed studies, international assessment reports, contacts with local experts). The latter is often the case for residential combustion of wood fuels (accounting for non-commercial fuel use), open burning of agricultural residues, and gas flaring.

The CLE scenario reflects the continuation of current legislation on energy use, energy efficiency, and climate mitigation, as described in the World Energy Outlook 2018's New Policies Scenario (IEA, 2018[2]). In addition to these policies, the CLE scenario considers detailed inventories of national emission control legislation described thoroughly by Amman et al. (2018[7]). The policies and inventories included in the CLE scenario include all those in place in 2017. Therefore, recent zero-emission pledges and targets are not included in this scenario.

The MTFR scenario reflects efforts to reduce the emission of air pollutants through regulations, emission standards, and emission limits. Such reductions are achieved thanks to the deployment of existing best available techniques (BATs) in different sectors. In other words, the MTFR scenarios reflect the maximum mitigation potential that is possible in each sector. The GAINS model contains an inventory of technically-feasible and commercially-available measures that could cut emissions below the baseline projections, adding to the measures already in place and included in the CLE scenario. Hence, when compared to the CLE scenario, the MTFR policy scenarios entail higher emission reductions.

The MTFR scenario reflects the deployment of source- and region-specific technologies that can reduce the emissions of several pollutants. These include (1) end-of-pipe technologies such as filters, scrubbers and catalytic converters; (2) pollutant capture and recovery systems (e.g. addressing non-methane volatile organic compounds emissions from the solvent sector); (3) cleaner and more efficient solid fuels for stoves and boilers; and (4) measures to reduce ammonia and methane emissions in the agricultural sector.

The BATs included in the MTFR scenarios differ in the timing of deployment, which depends on their ease of implementation. For instance, some BATs can quickly complement existing technologies (e.g. end-of-pipe cleaning techniques), while others, which completely replace existing technologies, have a longer lifetime and require more complex changes (e.g. heating stoves replacement).

Box 2.2. The IEA's Sustainable Development Scenario

The SDS scenario takes into account climate change mitigation and energy transition policies. The SDS scenario describes a path for the global energy sector that is aligned with the mitigation targets established by the Paris Agreement – i.e. holding the increase in global temperature to "well below 2°C" and "pursuing efforts to limit [it] to 1.5°C" (UNFCCC, 2015[8]). The policies included in the SDS scenario also allow for the energy-related goals established by the United Nations' (UN) 2030 Agenda for Sustainable Development to be achieved. Most notably, the SDS scenario includes the policies needed to transform the energy sector in order to (1) achieve universal access to energy (SDG 7); (2) reduce the health impacts of air pollution (SDG 3); (3) tackle climate change (SDG 13); and (4) achieve universal access to clean water and sanitation (SDG 6).

The policy instruments needed to achieve these results are integrated into the SDS scenario and include carbon pricing, energy taxes and the removal of fossil fuel subsidies. All these instruments are implemented in the ENV-Linkages model. More specifically, in the SDS scenario, carbon prices increase over time, from USD 121.5 to USD 140 per tCO_2 in 2040, with differences across countries and sectors. In parallel, fossil fuel subsidies are gradually removed during the same period. In addition, the share of non-fossil power sources rises to 40% in 2040, accompanied by improvements in energy efficiency.[1] Energy efficiency is measured by the energy intensity of GDPs, which drops from 110 tonnes of oil equivalent (toe)/USD 1 000 in 2017 to 40 toe/USD 1 000 in 2040 at the global level (IEA, 2018[2]).

Source: (IEA, 2018[2]).

2.2. Modelling framework

This report takes a quantitative approach to assess the economic consequences of air pollution to 2050. The modelling framework is based on an impact pathway approach,[2] which includes multiple steps and requires the use of different techniques and models. The methodology relies on the modelling framework used for the OECD's CIRCLE project, as described in the OECD report "*The Economic Consequences of Outdoor Air Pollution*" (OECD, 2016[9]). The modelling framework used in this report links projections of (1) sectoral economic activities to (2) emissions of air pollutants, (3) concentrations of fine particulate matter and ground-level ozone, and finally to (4) the biophysical and (5) economic impacts of outdoor air pollution (Figure 2.1). The steps outlined in Figure 2.1 are repeated for each scenario outlined in Section 2.1.

This methodology relies on a suite of modelling tools. The main tool for analysing the economic consequences of air pollution in the different scenarios is the OECD computable general equilibrium model ENV-Linkages, described in Annex A (Chateau, Dellink and Lanzi, 2014[1]). This analysis is supported by results from the GAINS integrated assessment model of the International Institute for Applied Systems Analysis (IIASA), which provides projections of air pollutants, emission reduction potentials, and required investments in emission reduction technologies (Amann et al., 2011[3]; Höglund-Isaksson et al., 2020[4]; Winiwarter et al., 2018[5]; Klimont et al., 2017[6]). The global air quality source-receptor model TM5-FASST (Van Dingenen et al., 2018[10]) of the Joint Research Centre of the European Commission provides the link between emission projections and exposure to $PM_{2.5}$ and ground-level ozone.

Figure 2.1. Methodological steps

1) PROJECTIONS OF SECTORAL ACTIVITIES	• The OECD ENV-Linkages model provides projections of sectoral economic activities for 19 geographical regions.
2) PROJECTIONS OF AIR POLLUTANT EMISSIONS	• IIASA's GAINS model provides emission projections for 48 countries and regions, building on ENV-Linkages' economic projections.
3) PROJECTIONS OF CONCENTRATIONS OF AIR POLLUTANTS	• The EC JRC's TM5-FASST model uses emission projections to calculate grid-level concentrations for $PM_{2.5}$ and O_3.
4) PROJECTIONS OF THE BIOPHYSICAL IMPACTS OF OUTDOOR AIR POLLUTION	• Concentration-response functions, based on the Global Burden of Disease studies, provide projections of the health impacts of outdoor air pollution by country (e.g. numbers of deaths, cases of illnesses, work days lost), based on the country-average concentrations of $PM_{2.5}$ and O_3 obtained with the TM5-FASST model. • The EC JRC's TM5 FASST model provides projections of agricultural impacts (i.e. lost crop productivity) by country.
5) PROJECTIONS OF THE ECONOMIC CONSEQUENCES OF OUTDOOR AIR POLLUTION	• The OECD ENV-Linkages model calculates projections of the macroeconomic consequences of air pollution for Arctic Council countries, based on the projected biophysical impacts. • Projections of the welfare consequences of air pollution, resulting from mortality and morbidity, are quantified at the country level using non-market valuation techniques.

Source: based on OECD (2016[9]).

The models operate at different scales while sharing the same socio-economic baseline trends. Combining these models allows the economic consequences of air pollution to be calculated at the macroeconomic level, while accounting for pollution concentrations at the local level. Specifically, economic projections are provided for 19 aggregate regions, while emission levels are available for 48 regions, and pollutant concentrations are specified at a 1-degree grid-level (i.e. about 44 km^2). The five methodological steps and their models (Figure 2.1) are described in turn below:

1. The projections of ***sectoral economic activities*** are obtained with the OECD CGE model ENV-Linkages (Chateau, Dellink and Lanzi, 2014[1]). ENV-Linkages allows for the creation of detailed projections of sectoral and regional economic activities to 2050 for 19 global regions. These projections rely on a range of key assumptions, drivers and exogenous trends, including demographic and technological developments, as described in OECD (2019[11]). The economic projections underlying the five scenarios reflect the steady economic growth characterising OECD countries and faster economic growth characterising non-OECD economies[3] (OECD, 2019[11]). This difference in economic growth trends is due to the long-term convergence process of non-OECD countries towards the OECD's average income levels, conditional on country-specific circumstances. Annex A contains more details on the ENV-Linkages model.

2. The economic activities are then used to obtain projections of air pollution ***emissions*** to 2050. This is done using the GAINS model (Höglund-Isaksson et al., 2020[4]; Winiwarter et al., 2018[5]; Klimont et al., 2017[6]; Amann et al., 2011[3]). Although this technology-based model has high spatial and sectoral resolution, this report relies on more aggregate information. Specifically, the analysis in this report uses activity-specific emissions projections for 48 countries and regions.[4] The pollutants projected in this report are: black carbon, organic carbon, sulphur dioxide, nitrogen oxides, volatile organic compounds, nitrous oxide, carbon monoxide, and ammonia. Due to lack of data, the report

does not cover other pollutants that affect the Arctic region, such as mercury (AMAP/UN Environment, 2019[12]) and persistent organic pollutants (POPs) (AMAP, 2016[13]).

3. Projected emissions are then used to calculate atmospheric **concentrations** of $PM_{2.5}$ and ground-level ozone, relying on the Fast Scenario Screening Tool TM5-FASST, a global air quality source-receptor model developed by the European Commission's Joint Research Centre (EC-JRC) (Van Dingenen et al., 2018[10]). Based on the aggregate emission projections provided by GAINS, TM5-FASST provides grid-level concentrations of $PM_{2.5}$ and ground-level ozone on a 1-degree grid. These are used as an input to calculate the country-specific biophysical impacts of air pollution. In order to provide a comprehensive assessment of air pollutant concentrations, TM5-FASST completes emission projections with additional data on emission sources that are not covered in GAINS and ENV-Linkages. These include natural emission sources (desert dust and sea salt), as well as emissions from forest fires, which are obtained from the Coupled Model Intercomparison Project (CMIP) projections. The TM5-FASST model also provides population-weighted[5] concentrations of air pollutants by country, which serve as an indicator of human exposure to air pollution.

4. Pollutant concentrations are used to calculate the **biophysical impacts** of air pollution on human health and agriculture. The biophysical impacts are described by a range of indicators, including mortality, hospital admissions and crop productivity losses (see Annex A). Health impacts at the country level are obtained using concentration-response functions based on the results of the Global Burden of Disease project for $PM_{2.5}$ (Forouzanfar et al., 2015[14]) and ground-level ozone (Stanaway et al., 2018[15]) (see Annex B). There is evidence that some $PM_{2.5}$ and ground-level ozone precursor gases such as NO_2 have direct negative health effects (COMEAP, 2015[16]; EPA, 2016[17]). However, the lack of available data with global coverage reduced the possibilities to include the environmental impacts of these gases in the analysis. Finally, the agricultural impacts are calculated using the TM5-FASST model, which estimates the crop yield changes associated with ground-level ozone concentrations (Van Dingenen et al., 2018[10]; Van Dingenen et al., 2009[18]).

5. Finally, the **economic consequences** of air pollution policies are calculated, and distinguish between: (1) macroeconomic effects; and (2) the welfare improvements from reduced mortality and morbidity. Since this step is central to the main results on the economic consequences of air pollution policies, Section 2.3 presents additional details on the methodology used for the economic analysis.

The benefits of policy action are quantified as the difference in results between the policy scenarios and the baseline scenario.[6]

2.3. Quantifying the economic consequences of air pollution policies

This report quantifies the economic consequences of air pollution policies by drawing a distinction between two complementary effects (Figure 2.2):

1. Macroeconomic effects: how air pollution and air pollution policies affect economic growth.

2. Welfare improvements: the reduced mortality and incidence of illness that follow from better air quality when air pollution policies are implemented are presented in monetary values.

Figure 2.2. Schematic overview of the economic consequences of air pollution policies

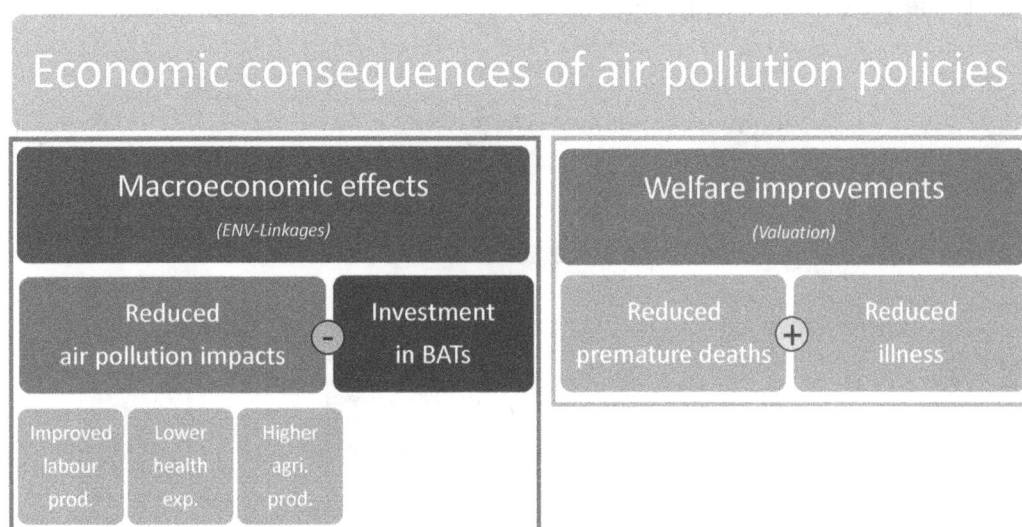

Macroeconomic effects

The macroeconomic effects quantified reflect the impact of air pollution policies on the economic system as a whole, including impacts on expenditures, factor productivity, production, consumption and trade. The indicator used for the macroeconomic effect is gross domestic product, as in previous OECD work on the costs of environmental inaction (OECD, 2015[19]; OECD, 2016[9]). While GDP is not a perfect indicator of the success of environmental policies (Paltsev and Capros, 2013[20]), it is a common indicator of economic growth.[7]

The macroeconomic effects of air pollution policies are calculated relying on the OECD ENV-Linkages model. The model considers both the benefits from the reduced air pollution impacts, and the costs of air pollution policies based on the necessary investment in best available techniques (BATs). The overall macroeconomic effect of policy action therefore depends on the relative size of such benefits and costs.

The modelling framework takes into account both direct and indirect effects. For instance, changes in households' health expenditures (direct costs) lead to changes in their consumption choices (indirect costs). Furthermore, in ENV-Linkages higher government spending encourages firms to increase investment, therefore leading to a positive effect on economic growth that partly offsets the initial costs.

The benefits of air pollution policies considered in ENV-Linkages result from reduced health expenditures, and improved labour and agricultural productivity (see Annex A for details). The input data to calculate these benefits are obtained by converting the biophysical impacts of air pollution (e.g. hospital admissions) into indicators that can be linked to ENV-Linkages' variables and regional aggregation (e.g. changes in health expenditures). For instance, health expenditures are calculated by multiplying the number of hospital admissions by the unit costs attributed to a single hospital admission.

The costs of the policy scenarios are quantified in ENV-Linkages, including as inputs the estimates of the investment and expenditures (hereafter, investment) in new technologies for firms and households provided by the GAINS model. In ENV-Linkages, the deployment of cleaner technologies is set to create additional capital stock that allows less-polluting production processes for each sector and for households.[8]

These input data on investment are higher in the MTFR-AC scenario than in the CLE scenario, with some differences across sectors and regions (Figure 2.3). In those regions or sectors where stringent emission controls are already in place, investments associated with the adoption of the BATs are already included in the CLE scenario, rendering the difference in investment between the two scenarios very small.

However, overall for Arctic Council countries, the MTFR-AC scenario sees substantial additional investments in the residential, energy and industry sectors, which have high potential for emission reductions.

Figure 2.3. Arctic Council country investment in BATs

Value in million USD, 2017 PPP exchange rates, 2050

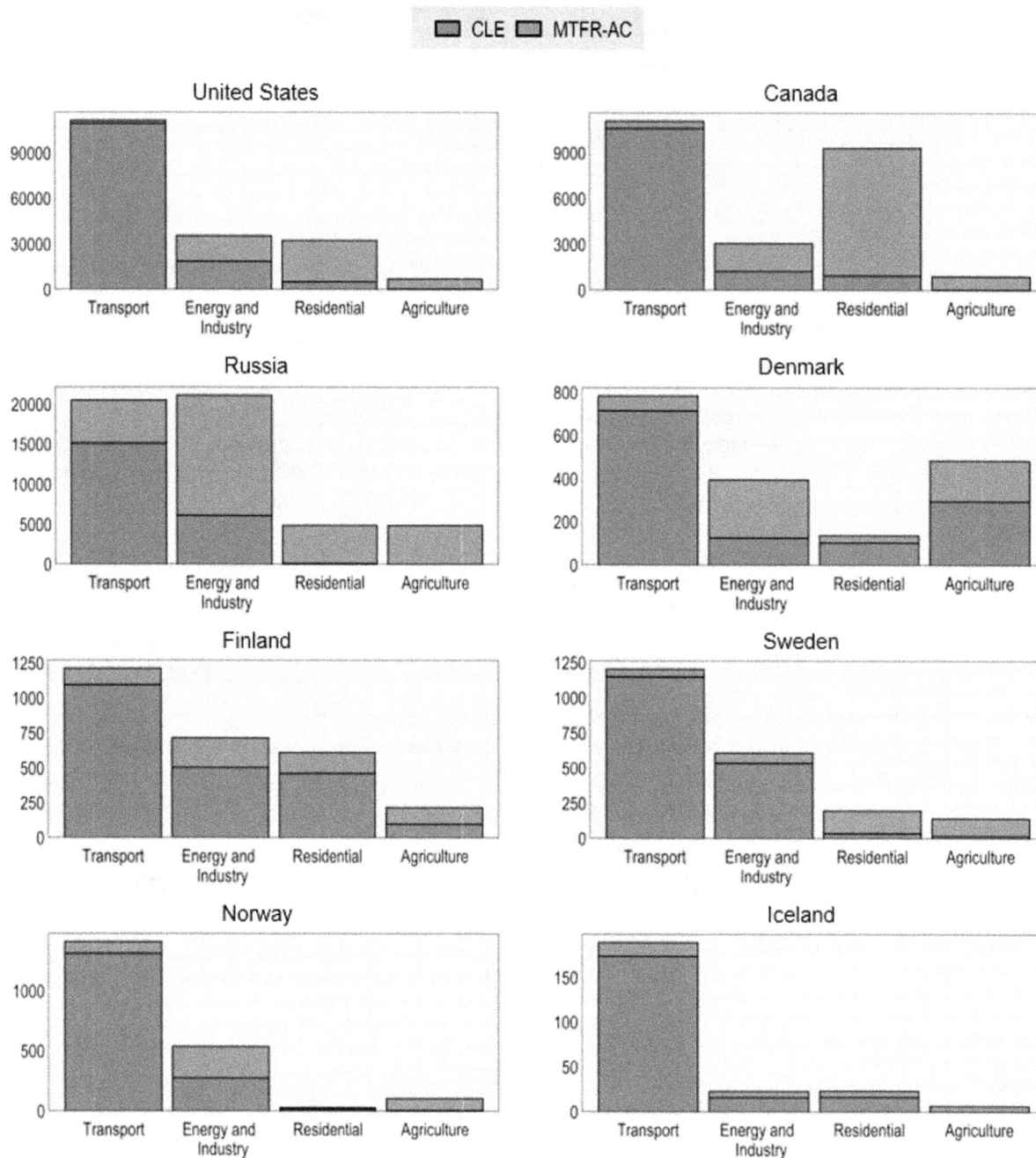

Note: In the graph, for each bar, the sum of grey and blue colours reflects MTFR-AC levels, while blue reflects CLE levels. Scales differ for each country. MTFR-AC: Maximum Technically Feasible Reduction in Arctic Council countries only; CLE: Current Legislation (Baseline); PPP: purchasing power parity.
Source: IIASA's GAINS model.

The differences in investment across sectors reflect the different costs and emission reduction potentials of the BATs, as well as the sectoral contribution to national emissions. Overall, two-thirds of the investment needed to achieve emission reductions under the CLE scenario are in the transport sector. This includes low-sulphur fuel for ocean ships, alongside end-of-pipe reductions that provide equivalent emission reductions in the case that high-sulphur fuel is used. The implementation of the best available techniques in the MTFR-AC scenario would require greater investments targeting the residential, energy, and agricultural sectors. In fact, about half of the additional investments under the MTFR-AC scenario are devoted to the residential sector, especially in Canada, the United States and the Nordic Arctic Council countries.[9] The energy and industry sector is the second by volume of additional investments under the MTFR-AC scenario, with most of these investments projected to take place in Russia.

Welfare improvements

The welfare improvements from reduced air pollution considered in this report include reduced air pollution-related mortality, and pain and suffering caused by illness. These effects are monetised using economic valuation techniques (see Annex B for details).

The welfare costs associated with mortality are calculated using the value of a statistical life (VSL), following previous OECD work (OECD, 2014[21]). This is a long-established metric, which can be quantified by aggregating individuals' willingness to pay (WTP) to secure a marginal reduction in mortality risk over a given timespan (Box 2.3) (OECD, 2012[22]; OECD, 2014[21]; Roy and Braathen, 2017[23]). The OECD environmental indicator database (OECD, 2020[24]) provides country-specific VSL values for adults for OECD member countries and some non-OECD economies. These VSLs, as well as values for other countries not covered by the database, are calculated using a benefit transfer methodology (Box 2.3).[10]

Alongside mortality, this report accounts for several morbidity impacts, including adult and childhood bronchitis, respiratory and cardiovascular illness, and asthma symptom days for children. While the healthcare costs included in the modelling analysis reflect the expenditures linked with each case of illness (e.g. the costs of medicines), the welfare costs of morbidity reflect the pain and suffering of each case of illness.

Welfare costs of morbidity impacts are monetised using previous work by the European Commission (Holland, 2014[25]), which established unit values for the welfare costs of each morbidity impact (reported in Annex B). Adjustment of morbidity welfare costs to specific countries is based on income, with the benefit transfer methodology used for mortality (Box 2.3).

Box 2.3. Valuing mortality using the value of a statistical life

One of the most common procedures to value risks to life in standard economic theory is the value of a statistical life (VSL) (OECD, 2006[26]). The VSL is derived from aggregating individuals' willingness to pay to secure a marginal reduction in mortality risks over a given timespan.

The VSL is most commonly elicited through stated preference techniques, although revealed preferences techniques are also used. OECD (2012[22]) describes the basic process for deriving a VSL from a stated preference survey. The VSL is not the value of an identified person's life, but rather an aggregation of individual values for small changes in risk of death (OECD, 2012[22]). As such, the total economic cost of the impact equals the VSL multiplied by the number of deaths; the economic benefit of a mitigating action becomes the same VSL multiplied by the number of lives saved (OECD, 2014[21]).

Since not all countries have a specific VSL value that they use for cost-benefit analysis, country-specific VSL values are established based on average national income, using a benefit transfer methodology (OECD, 2012[22]; OECD, 2014[21]). The key parameter in this methodology is the elasticity of income, which determines the extent to which the VSL changes according to different income levels. This approach allows for comprehensiveness and comparability across countries by using the same methodology and reference VSL. Furthermore, the VSL can be adapted over time to the income changes in the economic projections for each country. While the methodological choices and parameter values used could affect the magnitude of the results, the overall results and policy messages should not be affected. A sensitivity analysis to the values of the income elasticities is presented in OECD (2016[9]).

Mortality can also be valued using the "value of a life year lost" (VOLY). This technique calculates the number of "years of life lost" (YOLLs) from a specific risk, based on an estimated life expectancy, and then evaluates them by multiplying them by the VOLY. One issue with this technique is that the combination of counting YOLLs, rather than lives lost, means that the VOLY approach "explicitly places a lower value on reductions in mortality risk accruing to older populations with lower quality of life" (Hubbell, 2002[27]). There are also major complications in the robust estimation of YOLLs, and the extent to which existing country-specific life expectancy values can and should be used. Given the limitations of the use of VOLYs, and following OECD (2012[22]; 2014[21]), mortality is evaluated with the same VSL for all age groups in this report.

Notes

[1] ENV-Linkages does not fully incorporate the investment costs of energy-saving technologies in non-power industries, services and agricultural sectors, due to lack of information.

[2] Impact pathway assessments estimate environmental benefits and costs following the pathway from the sources of the environmental damage (in this case emissions of air pollutants), via changes in environmental quality (air quality), to physical impacts, before being expressed in monetary benefits and costs.

[3] The economic projections underlying the scenarios presented in this report do not consider the current COVID-19 pandemic and its effect on economic growth.

[4] The methodology used for create emission projections relies on the methodology used in the EU FP7 project on Low climate IMpact scenarios and the Implications of required Tight emission control Strategies (LIMITS) (Rao et al., 2016[29]), which was also used in previous OECD work (OECD, 2016[9]), and on the 30th Energy Modelling Forum (EMF30) modelling comparison exercise on the potential role of Short-Lived Climate Forcers (SLCF) mitigation in climate policy (Smith et al., 2020[30]), which also included the ENV-Linkages model (Chantret et al., 2020[31]; Harmsen et al., 2020[32]).

[5] The population-weighted average concentrations link population density to air pollution exposure. This indicator reflects the fact that areas with high population density imply higher exposure to air pollution, thereby capturing more accurately the exposure to air pollution in that country.

[6] In this modelling set up, the damage from air pollution affects economic output and growth. Therefore, in principle, for each scenario, emissions, concentration levels and impacts of air pollution should be re-assessed after considering the economic feedbacks from air pollution. This additional step should be repeated until convergence is reached between all steps in the framework. However, the reductions in economic activity due to the air pollution impacts for each scenario are limited and estimated to be around 1% of emissions in the baseline scenario (OECD, 2016[9]). Therefore, the second-order effect of lower emission projections on concentrations and impacts is very small, and can be ignored in the light of the uncertainties surrounding all calculations in this report.

[7] An alternative choice would have been to calculate the welfare impacts of the different scenarios in the ENV-Linkages model. Following previous OECD work (OECD, 2016[9]), the choice was made to highlight impacts on output and growth in the modelling analysis and to separately assess the welfare impacts of the policy scenarios with valuation techniques.

[8] This methodology is similar to the one used in the GEM-E3 model of the European Commission (Amann et al., 2017[28]).

[9] The Nordic Arctic Council countries are Denmark, Finland, Iceland, Norway and Sweden.

[10] The income elasticity used for the calculations is 0.8 for high-income countries, 0.9 for middle-income countries and 1 for low-income countries. See Annex B for a thorough description of the benefit-transfer methodology and for a discussion of the elasticity values.

References

Amann, M. et al. (2018), *Progress Towards the Achievement of the EU's Air Quality and Emissions Objectives*, International Institute for Applied Systems Analysis (IIASA), Laxenburg.   [7]

Amann, M. et al. (2011), "Cost-effective control of air quality and greenhouse gases in Europe: Modeling and policy applications", *Environmental Modelling & Software*, Vol. 26/12, pp. 1489-1501, http://dx.doi.org/10.1016/j.envsoft.2011.07.012.   [3]

Amann, M. et al. (2017), *Costs, Benefits and Economic Impacts of the EU Clean Air Strategy and their Implications on Innovation and Competitiveness*, International Institute for Applied Systems Analysis (IIASA), Laxenburg.   [28]

AMAP (2016), *AMAP Assessment 2015: Temporal Trends in Persistent Organic Pollutants in the Arctic. Arctic Monitoring and Assessment Programme (AMAP)*, AMAP, Tromsø.   [13]

AMAP/UN Environment (2019), *Technical Background Report for the Global Mercury Assessment 2018*, AMAP/UN Environment, Tromsø.   [12]

Chantret, F. et al. (2020), "Can better technologies avoid all air pollution damages to the global economy?", *Climatic Change*, Vol. 163/3, pp. 1463-1480.   [31]

Chateau, J., R. Dellink and E. Lanzi (2014), "An Overview of the OECD ENV-Linkages Model: Version 3", *OECD Environment Working Papers*, No. 65, OECD Publishing, Paris, https://dx.doi.org/10.1787/5jz2qck2b2vd-en.   [1]

COMEAP (2015), *Statement on the evidence for the effects of nitrogen dioxide on health.*, COMEAP, London, https://www.gov.uk/government/publications/nitrogen-dioxide-health-effects-of-exposure.   [16]

EPA (2016), *Integrated Science Assessment for Oxides of Nitrogen – Health Criteria*, Environmental Protection Agency, Washington DC, https://cfpub.epa.gov/ncea/isa/recordisplay.cfm?deid=310879.   [17]

Forouzanfar, M. et al. (2015), "Global, regional, and national comparative risk assessment of 79 behavioural, environmental and occupational, and metabolic risks or clusters of risks in 188 countries, 1990-2013: a systematic analysis for the Global Burden of Disease Study 2013", *The Lancet*, Vol. 386/10010, pp. 2287-2323, http://dx.doi.org/10.1016/S0140-6736(15)00128-2.   [14]

Harmsen, M. et al. (2020), "Taking some heat off the NDCs? The limited potential of additional short-lived climate forcers' mitigation", *Climatic change*, pp. 1443–1461.   [32]

Höglund-Isaksson, L. et al. (2020), "Technical potentials and costs for reducing global anthropogenic methane emissions in the 2050 timeframe –results from the GAINS model", *Environmental Research Communications*, Vol. 2/2, p. 025004, http://dx.doi.org/10.1088/2515-7620/ab7457.   [4]

Holland, M. (2014), *Cost-benefit Analysis of Final Policy Scenarios for the EU Clean Air Package*, Corresponding to IIASA TSAP Report No. 11, International Institute for Applied Systems Analysis (IIASA), Laxenburg, http://ec.europa.eu/environment/air/pdf/TSAP%20CBA.pdf (accessed on 9 March 2021). [25]

Hubbell, B. (2002), *Implementing QALYs in the Analysis of Air Pollution Regulations*, US Environmental Protection Agency, Washington, DC, https://www3.epa.gov/ttnecas1/workingpapers/ereqaly.pdf (accessed on 7 December 2020). [27]

IEA (2018), *World Energy Outlook 2018*, International Energy Agency, Paris, https://dx.doi.org/10.1787/weo-2018-en. [2]

Klimont, Z. et al. (2017), "Global anthropogenic emissions of particulate matter including black carbon", *Atmospheric Chemistry and Physics*, Vol. 17/14, pp. 8681-8723, http://dx.doi.org/10.5194/acp-17-8681-2017. [6]

OECD (2020), *Air quality and health: Mortality and welfare cost from exposure to air pollution (database)*, Statistics, OECD Environment, https://doi.org/10.1787/c14fb169-en (accessed on 3 November 2020). [24]

OECD (2019), *Global Material Resources Outlook to 2060: Economic Drivers and Environmental Consequences*, OECD Publishing, Paris, https://dx.doi.org/10.1787/9789264307452-en. [11]

OECD (2016), *The Economic Consequences of Outdoor Air Pollution*, OECD Publishing, Paris, https://dx.doi.org/10.1787/9789264257474-en. [9]

OECD (2015), *The Economic Consequences of Climate Change*, OECD Publishing, Paris, https://dx.doi.org/10.1787/9789264235410-en. [19]

OECD (2014), *The Cost of Air Pollution: Health Impacts of Road Transport*, OECD Publishing, Paris, https://dx.doi.org/10.1787/9789264210448-en. [21]

OECD (2012), *Mortality Risk Valuation in Environment, Health and Transport Policies*, OECD Publishing, Paris, https://dx.doi.org/10.1787/9789264130807-en. [22]

OECD (2006), *Cost-Benefit Analysis and the Environment: Recent Developments*, OECD Publishing, Paris, https://dx.doi.org/10.1787/9789264010055-en. [26]

Paltsev, S. and P. Capros (2013), "Cost concepts for climate change mitigation", *Climate Change Economics*, Vol. 04/supp01, p. 1340003, http://dx.doi.org/10.1142/s2010007813400034. [20]

Rao, S. et al. (2016), "A multi-model assessment of the co-benefits of climate mitigation for global air quality", *Environmental Research Letters*, Vol. 11/12, p. 124013, http://dx.doi.org/10.1088/1748-9326/11/12/124013. [29]

Roy, R. and N. Braathen (2017), "The rising cost of ambient air pollution thus far in the 21st century: results from the BRIICS and the OECD countries", *OECD Environment Working Papers*, No. 124, OECD Publishing, Paris, https://dx.doi.org/10.1787/d1b2b844-en. [23]

Smith, S. et al. (2020), *The Energy Modeling Forum (EMF)-30 study on short-lived climate forcers: introduction and overview*, Springer Science and Business Media B.V., http://dx.doi.org/10.1007/s10584-020-02938-5. [30]

Stanaway, J. et al. (2018), "Global, regional, and national comparative risk assessment of 84 behavioural, environmental and occupational, and metabolic risks or clusters of risks for 195 countries and territories, 1990–2017: a systematic analysis for the Global Burden of Disease Study 2017", *The Lancet*, Vol. 392/10159, pp. 1923-1994, http://dx.doi.org/10.1016/s0140-6736(18)32225-6. [15]

UNFCCC (2015), *"Paris Agreement", United Nations Framework Convention on Climate Change*, (UNFCCC), New York, https://unfccc.int/sites/default/files/english_paris_agreement.pdf. (accessed on 1 December 2020). [8]

Van Dingenen, R. et al. (2018), "TM5-FASST: a global atmospheric source–receptor model for rapid impact analysis of emission changes on air quality and short-lived climate pollutants", *Atmospheric Chemistry and Physics*, Vol. 18, pp. 16173-16211, https://doi.org/10.5194/acp-18-16173-2018. [10]

Van Dingenen, R. et al. (2009), "The global impact of ozone on agricultural crop yields under current and future air quality legislation", *Atmospheric Environment*, Vol. 43/3, pp. 604-618, http://dx.doi.org/10.1016/j.atmosenv.2008.10.033. [18]

Winiwarter, W. et al. (2018), "Technical opportunities to reduce global anthropogenic emissions of nitrous oxide", *Environmental Research Letters*, Vol. 13/1, p. 014011, http://dx.doi.org/10.1088/1748-9326/aa9ec9. [5]

3. Air quality improvements and health benefits of air pollution policies

This chapter presents the projected emissions and concentrations of air pollutants in Arctic Council countries to 2050 under two scenarios: the baseline Current Legislation scenario (CLE) and a policy scenario reflecting the Maximum Technically Feasible Reduction in emissions of air pollutants in Arctic Council countries (MTFR-AC). The chapter begins by outlining the projections for the key air pollutants: sulphur dioxide, nitrogen oxides, black carbon, organic carbon, carbon monoxide, non-methane volatile organic compounds and ammonia. It then looks at projections for fine particulate matter and ground-level ozone concentrations. Finally, the chapter quantifies projections of the health impacts of the scenarios in terms of morbidity and mortality reductions, highlighting the benefits of policy-induced technical changes for air quality and human health.

3.1. Projections of key air pollutant emissions

Based on existing policies, emissions in Arctic Council countries are projected to decrease in the coming decades, even in the absence of additional policy action (baseline CLE scenario).[1] Altogether, under the baseline scenario, by the middle of the century Arctic Council countries are projected to see emissions fall by 25% to 40%, depending on the pollutant[2] (Figure 3.1). Emissions of SO_2 are projected to decrease by 40% by 2025 and to then decrease only marginally by 2050. Strong abatement of SO_2 emissions has already taken place prior to 2013, so by 2025 most of the abatement potential is exhausted. Emissions of other pollutants are projected to decrease more substantially over time. However, according to the GAINS model projections, Arctic Council countries are projected to achieve an aggregate BC emission reduction of 21% by 2025 compared to 2013 in the baseline scenario, coming close to their aspirational collective target of reducing these emissions by 25-33%.[3]

Although emissions are set to decline in Arctic Council countries even in the absence of additional policies, the implementation of policies to deploy the best available techniques could achieve much greater air quality improvements (Figure 3.1). Indeed, under the scenario of Maximum Technically Feasible Reduction in Arctic Council countries (MTFR-AC), NO_x, SO_2, and CO emissions are projected to decrease by 60% by the middle of the century. In addition, the MTFR-AC scenario would also allow a collective reduction of BC emissions by 65% by 2025, thus significantly exceeding the countries' reduction target.

Figure 3.1. Projected emissions of key air pollutants in Arctic Council countries

Index with respect to 2013 (Index =1 in 2013)

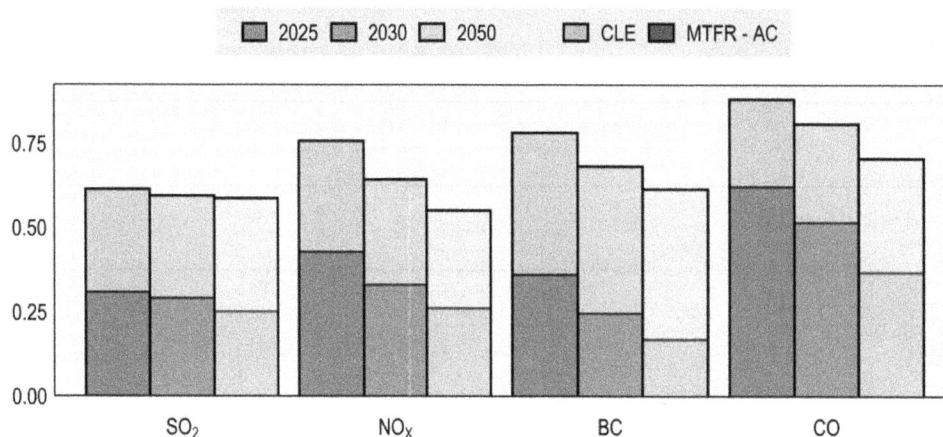

Note: For each bar in this figure, the sum of dark and light colours represents emission levels under CLE, while dark colours alone represent emission levels under MTFR-AC. CLE: Current Legislation baseline scenario; MTFR-AC: Maximum Technically Feasible Reduction in Arctic Council countries scenario.
Source: IIASA's GAINS model.

StatLink ᴍᴵˢᴸᴱ https://stat.link/zk32fo

However, BC emission projections for individual countries display large differences (Figure 3.2). With current policies, the largest emission reductions in percentage change compared to 2013 levels would take place in Nordic countries, which are projected to halve their emissions by 2025 under the CLE scenario. By 2025, most Arctic Council countries are projected to be close to meeting their emission reduction potential for several pollutants, with current legislation. As a consequence, the additional emission reductions under the MTFR-AC scenario are relatively small. Conversely, Russia[4] is projected to experience larger emission reductions under the MTFR-AC scenario.

Figure 3.2. Projected black carbon emissions by Arctic Council country

Kt/year, 2013 and 2025

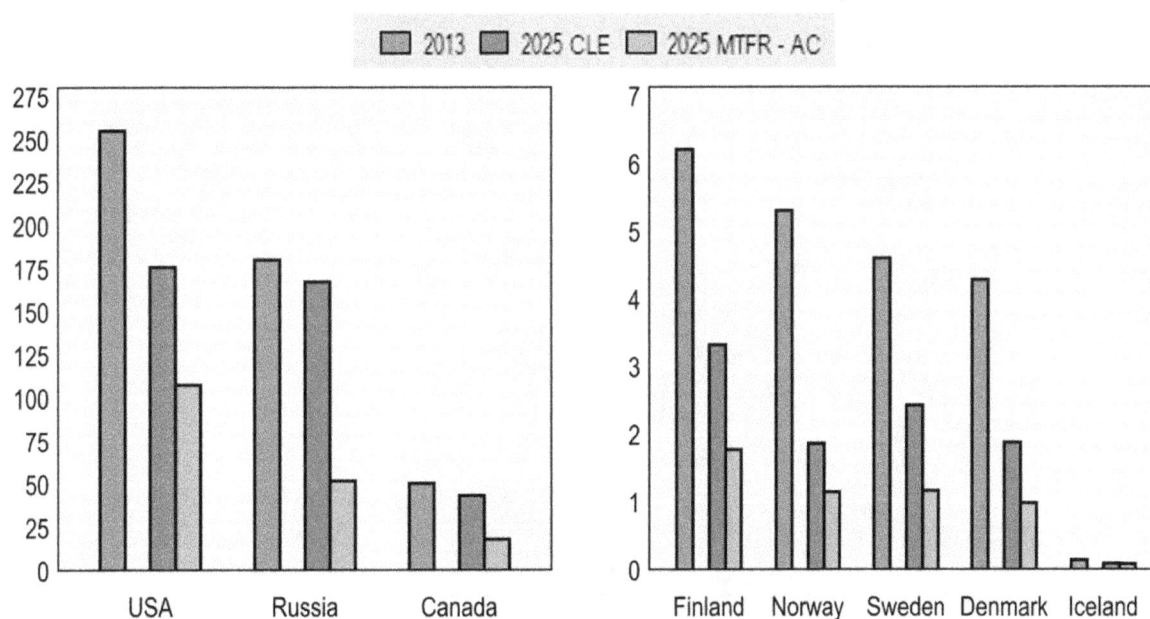

Note: Kt/year: thousand tonnes per year. The two graphs use different scales, as Nordic countries have lower emission levels.
Source: IIASA's GAINS model.

StatLink ᴹˢᴾ https://stat.link/tr5yun

The aggregate emission reductions result from different sectoral contributions to overall abatement, which vary by pollutant. Most abatement of SO_2 and NO_x takes place in the energy and industrial sectors, whereas emissions of CO are mostly reduced in the transport sectors. BC emissions are projected to be reduced most in the residential sector (Figure 3.3). These sectoral emission reductions are not necessarily proportional to the sector-specific investments and they lead to reduced emissions for different pollutants (Figure 3.3). The benefits of the sectoral investments in terms of emission reductions depend on the cost of the BATs and their efficiency. For example, emission reductions in the residential sectors are more costly than in other sectors, but they are also most efficient in reducing black carbon emissions. Furthermore, these costs may fall on different stakeholders depending on the sector, while the benefits may be seen elsewhere. For example, reducing residential wood-burning emissions can be costly, and households might only benefit marginally from improved air quality. While there are differences in costs and resulting emission reductions of each sector, a full cost-benefit analysis by sector is beyond the scope of this report.

Figure 3.3. Projected sectoral investment in BATs and emission reductions in Arctic Council countries

Percentage of emission reduced by sector for each gas, 2050 (left axis)
Billion USD, 2017 PPP exchange rates, 2050 (right axis)

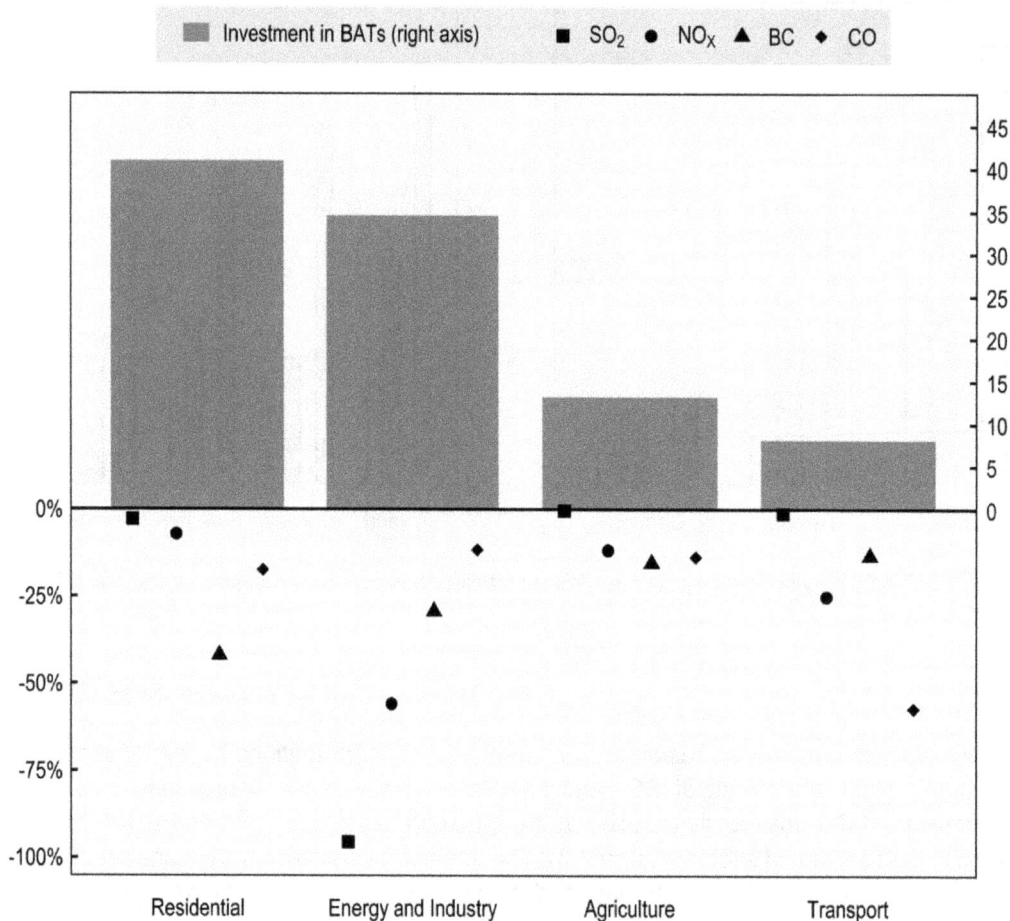

Note: BATs: best available technologies; BC: black carbon; CO: carbon monoxide; NO_x: nitrogen oxides; PPP: purchasing power parity; SO_2: sulphur dioxide
Source: IIASA's GAINS model.

StatLink ᵐˢᴾ https://stat.link/wmbjry

3.2. Projections of atmospheric concentrations of $PM_{2.5}$ and ground-level ozone

Thanks to the declining emission trends in Arctic Council countries, atmospheric concentrations of $PM_{2.5}$ are projected to decrease even in the absence of further policy action (Figure 3.4, Panel A). However, by 2050 the additional policies in the MTFR-AC scenario would lead to an even greater improvement in air quality, especially in urban areas[5] (Figure 3.4, Panel B). Furthermore, under the CLE scenario only a limited area in the north of the Arctic has $PM_{2.5}$ concentration levels close to zero, while in the MTFR-AC scenario, a larger part of the Arctic would have near-zero emissions.

Figure 3.4. Projected concentrations of PM2.5 in Arctic Council countries

Annual average anthropogenic PM$_{2.5}$ concentrations, µg/m^3, 2050

Panel A. CLE scenario

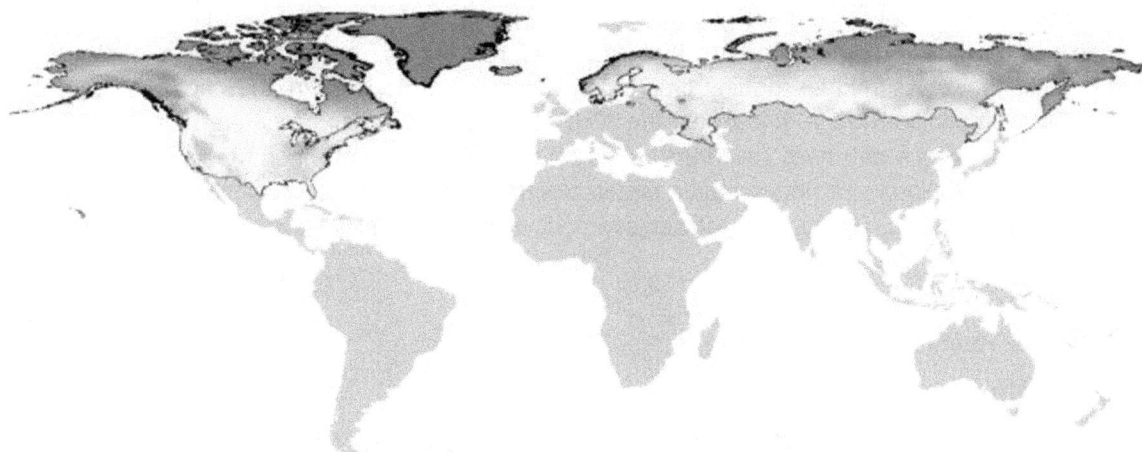

Panel B. MTFR-AC scenario

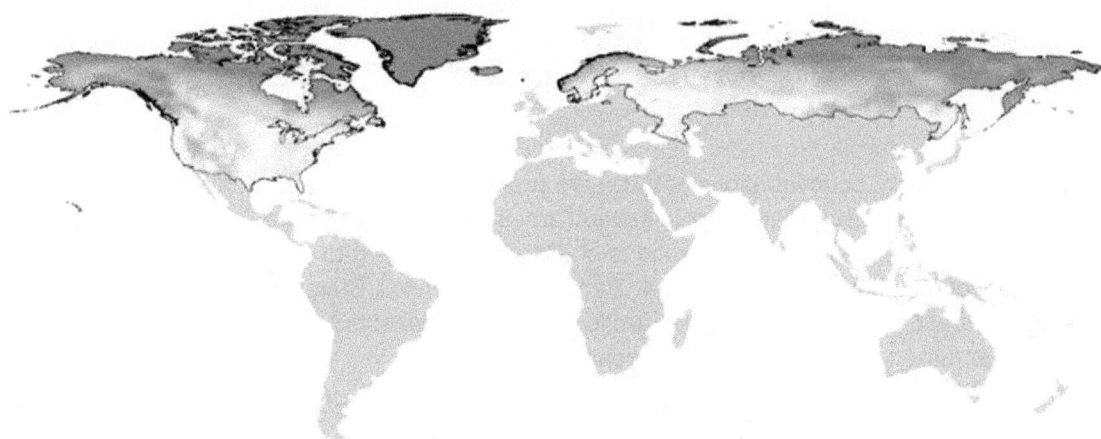

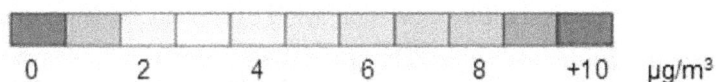

| 0 | 2 | 4 | 6 | 8 | +10 | µg/m^3 |

Note: µg/m3: micrograms per cubic metre.
Source: EC-JRC's TM5-FASST model.

To better understand these air quality improvements, the concentration levels can be compared to the World Health Organisation's (WHO) Air Quality Guidelines (Box 3.1) (WHO, 2005[1]). The guidelines for PM$_{2.5}$ indicate a target value of 10 µg/m^3 average annual concentrations. However, there could still be negative health impacts from air pollution below this level. The calculations of the health risks linked with exposure to PM$_{2.5}$ used in this report rely on the Global Burden of Disease's Integrated Exposure-

Response functions (Cohen et al., 2018[2]; Burnett et al., 2014[3]), which set the zero risk threshold at 2.5 µg/m³ concentrations of PM2.5 (see Annex B).

Box 3.1. WHO guidelines on outdoor air quality

The WHO air quality guidelines provide guidance on exposure levels to air pollutants that are dangerous to human health. Relevant to this report are the guidelines for particulate matter and ground-level ozone. These guidelines were issued for the first time in 1987; they were updated in 2005 and are currently under revision. In addition to the guidelines, the WHO has also issued some "interim targets" (Table 3.1). The interim targets can be considered as intermediate objectives to incrementally improve air quality up to the guideline value. Intermediate targets are particularly useful for regions that are affected by more severe pollution, where a direct achievement of the air quality guidelines would be more difficult.

Table 3.1. WHO guidelines and interim targets for particulate matter and ground-level ozone

	PM_{10} (µg/m³) (annual concentration)	$PM_{2.5}$ (µg/m³) (annual concentration)	O_3 (µg/m³) (8-hour daily mean)
Interim target-1 (IT-1)	70	35	160
Interim target-2 (IT-2)	50	24	
Interim target-3 (IT-3)	30	15	
Air quality guideline (AQG)	20	10	100

Note: WHO guidelines list only one interim target for ground-level ozone concentrations.
Source: (WHO, 2005[1]), WHO Air Quality Guidelines for Particulate Matter, Ozone, Nitrogen Dioxide and Sulfur Dioxide.

Under the CLE scenario, concentrations of PM2.5 are projected to remain above the levels recommended by the WHO's Air Quality Guideline value in several areas (red areas in Figure 3.4, Panel A). However, in the MTFR-AC scenario, average concentrations of PM2.5 are projected to fall below the guideline value in Arctic Council countries by 2050 (Figure 3.4, Panel B). The United States and Russia still have higher levels of concentrations of PM2.5 than other Arctic Council countries, but, on average, they also have the largest improvements compared to the CLE scenario.

This improvement in air quality would reduce the number of people exposed to fine particles at concentrations above the WHO guidelines (Figure 3.4). According to the projections for 2050, with existing policies (the CLE scenario), 8% of the population living in Arctic Council countries would be exposed to concentration levels of PM2.5 above the WHO guidelines. However, in the MTFR-AC scenario only 1% would be exposed to these concentrations. This decrease is equivalent to a change from 18 million people being exposed to concentrations higher than the WHO guidelines in the CLE scenario to 1 million people in the MTFR-AC scenario. Furthermore, while under the CLE scenario only 16% of the population would be exposed to very low PM2.5 air pollution levels (with concentrations below 2.5 micrograms per cubic metre), under the MTFR-AC scenario this share of the population would rise to more then 50%.

Figure 3.5. Projected exposure to PM$_{2.5}$ concentrations in Arctic Council countries

Percentage of population exposed to different concentration levels, 2050

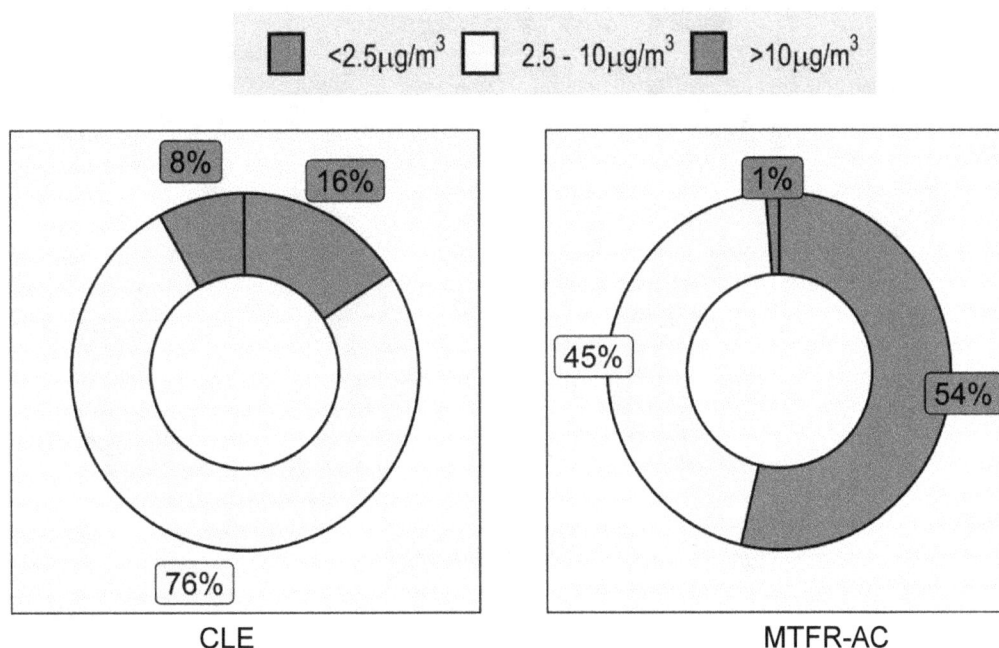

| ■ <2.5µg/m^3 | ☐ 2.5 - 10µg/m^3 | ■ >10µg/m^3 |

CLE: 8%, 16%, 76%

MTFR-AC: 1%, 45%, 54%

CLE   MTFR-AC

Note: The highest threshold (10 µg/m^3) refers to the WHO Air Quality Guidelines, while the lowest (2.5 µg/m^3) to the threshold under which the Global Burden of Disease functions consider that PM$_{2.5}$ pollution does have significant health impacts. µg/m^3: micrograms per cubic metre. *Source*: EC-JRC's TM5-FASST model.

StatLink 📊 https://stat.link/14gq3w

In the CLE scenario, the seasonal average of daily maximum eight-hour concentrations of ground-level ozone is projected to increase to 2050 in all the Arctic Council countries. However, with additional policy action in the MTFR-AC scenario, ground-level ozone concentrations would slightly decrease in 2050, with stronger effects in the United States and Russia (Figure 3.6).[6] Compared to PM$_{2.5}$, the longer lifetime of ground-level ozone in the atmosphere makes it more dependent on historical emissions, weather conditions and emissions from neighbouring countries. Thus, even when Arctic Council countries reduce emissions of ground-level ozone precursor gases, the decrease in concentrations is limited.

Figure 3.6. Projected concentrations of ground-level ozone in Arctic Council countries

Seasonal (6 months) average of daily maximum 8-hour mean, ppb, 2050

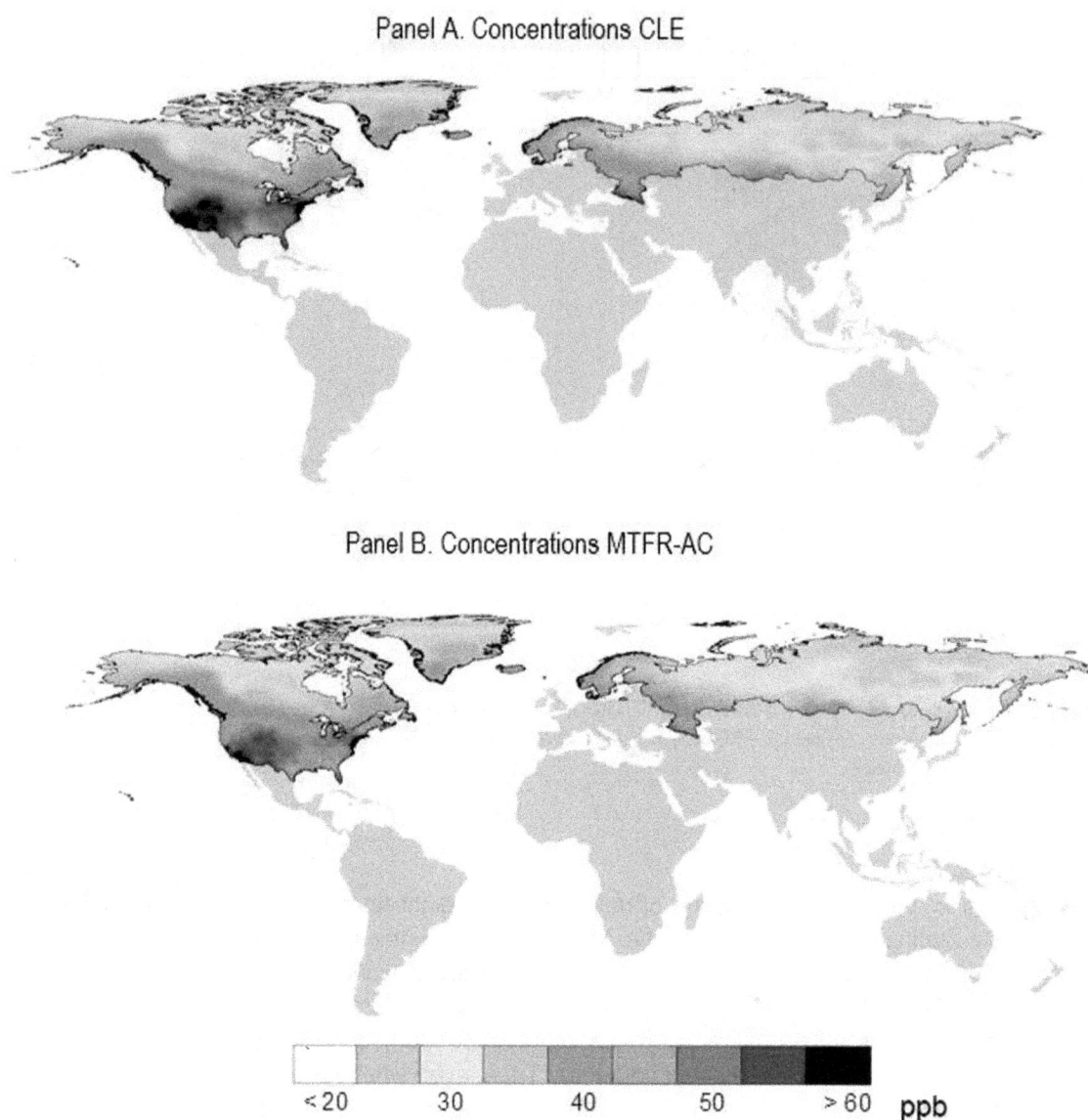

Panel A. Concentrations CLE

Panel B. Concentrations MTFR-AC

Note: ppb: parts per billion.
Source: EC-JRC's TM5-FASST model.

3.3. Projections of the health impacts of PM2.5 and ground-level ozone pollution

In Arctic Council countries, fine particulate matter and ground-level ozone are responsible for more than 200 000 deaths every year. Despite the projected improvement in air quality in Arctic Council countries by the middle of the century, projected population growth and urbanisation mean that, in the absence of additional policy action, an increasing number of people are set to be exposed to air pollution in the region. Therefore, the total number of deaths linked to exposure to PM2.5 and ground-level ozone[7] in Arctic Council countries is projected to remain approximately constant over time. As illustrated in Figure 3.7, under the

CLE scenario, deaths attributable to these air pollutants in the Arctic Council region are projected to decrease from 225 000 in 2025 to 216 000 in 2050.[8]

The full deployment of the best available techniques to reduce air pollution in Arctic Council countries (MTFR-AC scenario) could result in at least 61 000 fewer deaths from $PM_{2.5}$ and ground-level ozone every year by 2025 compared to the current policies scenario; 70 000 fewer deaths per year by 2030 and 80 000 fewer per year by 2050 (Figure 3.7). Overall, by the middle of the century, 4 out of 10 air pollution-related deaths could be avoided. While this reduction in mortality is a positive outcome of the air pollution policies, it is not as large as it could be given the large size of the emissions reductions. Air pollution causes mortality and illness even at low levels and, despite the emission reductions, air pollution persists especially in urban areas.

Figure 3.7. Projected mortality due to $PM_{2.5}$ and ground-level ozone in Arctic Council countries

Thousands deaths per year

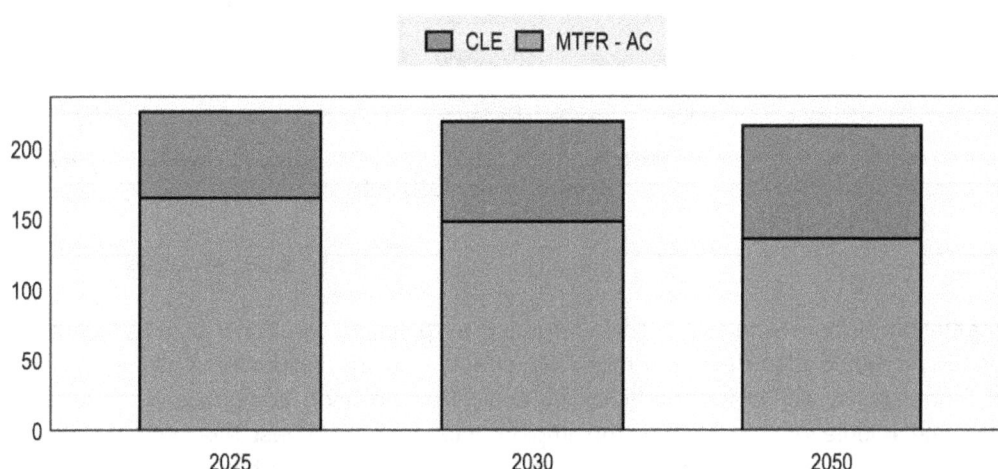

Notes: In the graph, for each bar, the sum of grey and blue colours reflect CLE levels, while the grey colour alone reflects MTFR-AC levels. While this report presents a single value estimate for the health impacts, there is an uncertainty range, which is discussed in (OECD, 2016[4]). *Source*: ENV-Linkages' model projections, based on Global Burden of Disease (GBD, 2018[5]).

StatLink ⛭ https://stat.link/54yd9i

The projected reductions in air pollution-driven mortality vary significantly across countries (Figure 3.8). For example, the benefits experienced by Iceland are very small, as the country is projected to already nearly reach its full emission reduction potential under the CLE scenario. Conversely, most of the other Arctic Council countries are projected to experience substantial benefits. These benefits are also projected to increase over time. Thus, by 2050, the deployment of the best available techniques included in the MTFR-AC scenario could reduce 36% of pollution-driven mortality in most Arctic Council countries (Figure 3.8).

Figure 3.8. Projected mortality due to PM$_{2.5}$ and ground-level ozone by Arctic Council country

Number of deaths per year

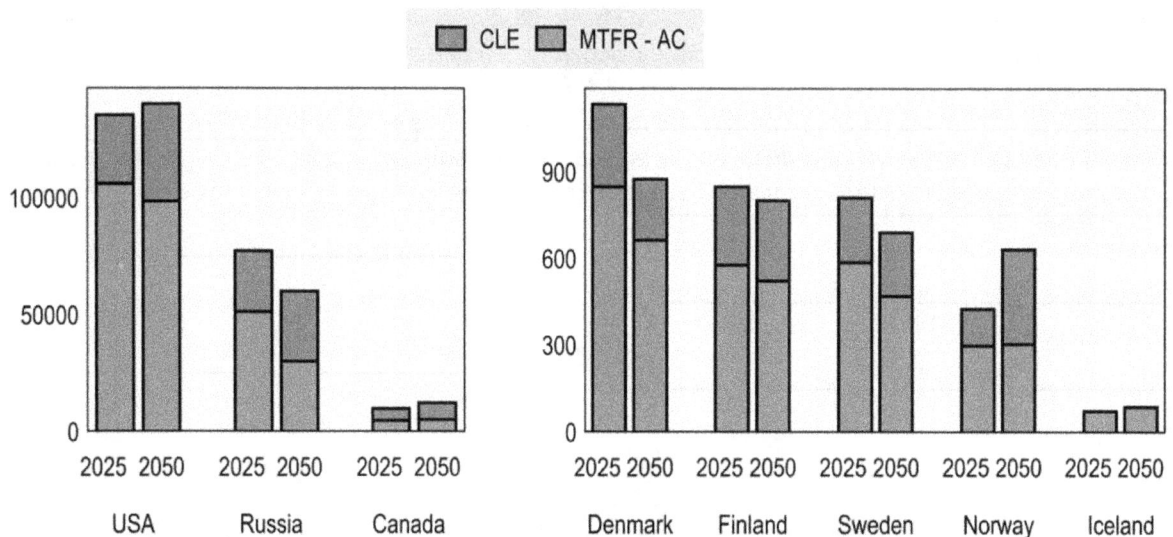

Note: In the graph, for each bar, the sum of grey and blue colours reflect CLE levels, while the grey colour only reflects MTFR-AC levels.
Source: ENV-Linkages' model projections, based on Global Burden of Disease (GBD, 2018[5]).

StatLink https://stat.link/4vp6zq

The implementation of more stringent policies targeting air pollution would not only reduce air pollution-related mortality, it would also decrease morbidity effects (i.e. the incidence of illness).[9] While in the absence of further policy action the morbidity impacts of air pollution are projected to remain roughly constant until the middle of the century, the implementation of the best available techniques would significantly reduce the incidence of illness, with the most significant benefits resulting after 2025 (Table 3.2). For example, the avoided days of children suffering from asthma symptoms would amount to 2.2 million in 2025 and to 3 million in 2050. Furthermore, by the middle of the century, the MTFR-AC scenario would avoid 33 million lost workdays every year. Similarly, by 2050, air pollution-related hospital admissions are projected to fall by 60% compared to the CLE scenario for the same year.

Table 3.2. Projected avoided morbidity impacts in Arctic Council countries

	2025	2030	2050
Respiratory diseases (thousands of cases)			
Bronchitis in children aged 6 to 12	232	303	330
Chronic bronchitis in adults	67	87	95
Asthma symptom days (millions of days)			
Asthma symptoms in children aged 5 to 19	2.2	2.8	3
Healthcare costs (thousands of admissions)			
Equivalent hospital admissions	74	92	100
Restricted activity days (millions of days)			
Lost working days	23	30	33
Restricted activity days	98	128	139

Note: The reductions reflect the comparison between the MTFR-AC scenario and the CLE scenario.
Source: ENV-Linkages' model projections and Holland (2014[6]), based on Global Burden of Disease (GBD, 2018[5]; Institute for Health Metrics and Evaluation (IHME), 2018[7]).

The decrease of morbidity impacts will result in healthcare savings for Arctic Council countries. Healthcare savings calculated in this report are attributed to fewer cases of bronchitis in children and adults and a reduction in hospital admissions. In 2025, reduced air pollution from the implementation of policy action promoting deployment of BATs will save USD 1.3 billion (2017 PPP) in health expenditures, rising to USD 1.8 billion (2017 PPP) by 2050.

Notes

[1] The emission projections presented in this section and used in this report rely on the GAINS model's scenarios developed for the European Union-funded Action on Black Carbon in the Arctic (Klimont et al., forthcoming[9]). These scenarios provide a consistent framework to assess emission projections. The country-specific emission projections used might differ from projections developed individually by each country (see Box 2.1, Chapter 2).

[2] All emission reductions in this section are calculated with reference to 2013 levels, unless otherwise specified.

[3] This result is specific to the simulations produced for this report. Other assessments might lead to different results. Specifically, this result differs from the projected emission reductions submitted by individual Arctic Council countries to the Expert Group on Black Carbon and Methane (EGBCM), as reported in the 2019 EGBCM Summary of Progress and Recommendations (Arctic Council, 2019[10]). According to the EGBCM's report, Arctic Council countries are projected to achieve a 23% reduction by 2025, assuming no change in emissions from Russia since 2013. Russia has not submitted individual projections, which makes it difficult to assess progress on BC emission reductions.

[4] In the 2015 and 2017 national reporting, all Arctic Council countries have some level of BC emission data available. However, Russia only reported BC emissions to the Arctic Council in 2015 and has not provided BC inventory data to the Convention on Long-Range Transboundary Air Pollution. The absence of routine reporting by Russia represents a particularly significant gap in monitoring BC emissions that directly affect the Arctic (AMAP, 2019[8]). Nevertheless, there are independent BC emission inventories for Arctic Council and Observer countries, such as the GAINS model emission estimates used in this report. These include source- and region-specific technology characteristics (Klimont et al., 2017[11]).

[5] Urban areas are visible as the red areas in Figure 3.4, Panel A.

[6] These concentration levels cannot be compared directly to the WHO's Air Quality Guidelines (100 µg/m^3) as the guidelines are relative to a daily average, and not to a seasonal average. This is because, while there is evidence of the effect of peak exposure to ground-level ozone on health, there is not enough evidence on the effects of long-term exposure, which would justify using a yearly average (WHO, 2005[1]).

[7] Mortality figures presented in this report include deaths due to stroke; ischaemic heart disease; tracheal, bronchus and lung cancer; chronic obstructive pulmonary disease; diabetes mellitus type 2; and lower respiratory infections resulting from exposure to $PM_{2.5}$ concentrations only.

[8] See Annex B for the methodology for calculating air pollution-related mortality.

[9] This report focuses on a subset of health impacts that can be quantified at the global level. These include chronic bronchitis in adults, acute bronchitis and asthma symptoms in children, lost workdays, restricted activity days and hospital admissions. Other illnesses (e.g. impacts on fertility and birth weight) could not be quantified. See 1Part IAnnex B for the methodology for calculating the morbidity impacts of air pollution.

References

AMAP (2019), *Review of Reporting Systems for National Black Carbon Emissions Inventories*, https://www.amap.no/documents/doc/eua-bca-technical-report-2/1780 (accessed on 16 December 2019). [8]

Arctic Council (2019), *Expert Group on Black Carbon and Methane - Summary of Progress and Reccomendations*, https://oaarchive.arctic-council.org/handle/11374/2411 (accessed on 8 December 2020). [10]

Burnett, R. et al. (2014), "An integrated risk function for estimating the global burden of disease attributable to ambient fine particulate matter exposure", *Environmental Health Perspectives*, Vol. 122/4, pp. 397-403, http://dx.doi.org/10.1289/ehp.1307049. [3]

Cohen, A. et al. (2018), "Global estimates of mortality associated with long-term exposure to outdoor fine particulate matter", *Proceedings of the National Academy of Sciences*, Vol. 115/38, pp. 9592-9597, http://dx.doi.org/10.1073/pnas.1803222115. [2]

GBD (2018), *Global Burden of Disease Study 2017: All cause Mortality and Life Expectancy 1950-2017, Global Burden of Disease Collaborative Network.*, Seattle, United States: Institute for Health Metrics and Evaluation (IHME). [5]

Holland, M. (2014), *Cost-benefit Analysis of Final Policy Scenarios for the EU Clean Air Package*, Corresponding to IIASA TSAP Report No. 11, International Institute for Applied Systems Analysis (IIASA), Laxenburg, http://ec.europa.eu/environment/air/pdf/TSAP%20CBA.pdf (accessed on 9 March 2021). [6]

Institute for Health Metrics and Evaluation (IHME) (2018), *Global Life Expectancy, All-Cause Mortality, and Cause-Specific Mortality Forecasts 2016-2040*, Seattle, United States: Institute for Health Metrics and Evaluation (IHME), https://vizhub.healthdata.org/gbd-foresight/ (accessed on 2 December 19). [7]

Klimont, Z. et al. (forthcoming), "Global scenarios of anthropogenic emissions of air pollutants: ECLIPSE". [9]

Klimont, Z. et al. (2017), "Global anthropogenic emissions of particulate matter including black carbon", *Atmospheric Chemistry and Physics*, Vol. 17/14, pp. 8681-8723, http://dx.doi.org/10.5194/acp-17-8681-2017. [11]

OECD (2016), *The Economic Consequences of Outdoor Air Pollution*, OECD Publishing, Paris, https://dx.doi.org/10.1787/9789264257474-en. [4]

WHO (2005), *WHO Air quality guidelines for particulate matter, ozone, nitrogen dioxide and sulfur dioxide*, http://apps.who.int/iris/bitstream/handle/10665/69477/WHO_SDE_PHE_OEH_06.02_eng.pdf;jsessionid=DFDA9BAE204770F4BA4490E3A309C33A?sequence=1 (accessed on 8 December 2020). [1]

4. Economic consequences of air pollution policies

This chapter presents the economic consequences of air pollution policies including both macroeconomic and welfare effects. The macroeconomic effects cover the benefits from reduced air pollution and the costs of the policy-induced deployment of best available techniques. These effects are presented in terms of GDP and with a breakdown of costs and benefits by region. The chapter also estimates the economic impacts of welfare improvements arising from improved health, specifically lower mortality and morbidity.

4.1. Macroeconomic effects

There are both macroeconomic costs and benefits associated with reducing air pollution. The biophysical impacts of air pollution can affect sectoral productivity and consumption choices, resulting in what are referred to as "market costs". In particular, air pollution leads to lower labour and agricultural productivity and higher health expenditures. When air quality improves, the market costs of air pollution decrease, with resulting macroeconomic benefits. However, improving air quality is not free of cost. The emission reductions considered in this report result from policies that stimulate investments in the best available techniques (BATs) to abate emissions. Investments in new technologies entail additional expenditures for firms in a variety of sectors, as well as for households (e.g. for acquiring and installing pollution filters), which result in macroeconomic costs. The market costs of air pollution and the investments in BATs also have indirect effects, which can be either negative or positive (e.g. lower disposable income due to expenditure on BATs versus higher output thanks to increased labour productivity). Together, these lead to a net "macroeconomic effect" calculated as an overall change in GDP, as described in Section 2.3.

The MTFR-AC scenario suggests that by 2025, Arctic Council countries' actions to improve air quality would have no significant impacts on economic growth. Overall, in these countries in the short term, the macroeconomic effect of the air pollution policies considered in the MTFR-AC scenario is minimal and even slightly positive (Figure 4.1). The economic benefits from the reduced market impacts of air pollution in Arctic Council countries in 2025 amount to 0.2% of their aggregate GDP, while the total cost of adopting BATs to reduce air pollution amounts to 0.1% of their aggregate GDP.

In the longer term, the economic benefits from improved air quality keep increasing. The costs of technological investments also increase at the same time, as newer – and thus more expensive – technological options are adopted. As firms and households in Arctic Council countries incur additional expenditures, several economic sectors are likely to lose out to competitors from countries that are not adopting any additional air pollution policies. As a result, the macroeconomic effects of reducing air pollution are projected to become slightly negative by 2050. Nevertheless, these effects are very small and overall the air pollution policies reflected in this modelling analysis can be considered GDP-neutral.

Figure 4.1. Overall GDP impact of adopting BATs to reduce air pollution in Arctic Council countries

% GDP in the MTFR-AC scenario

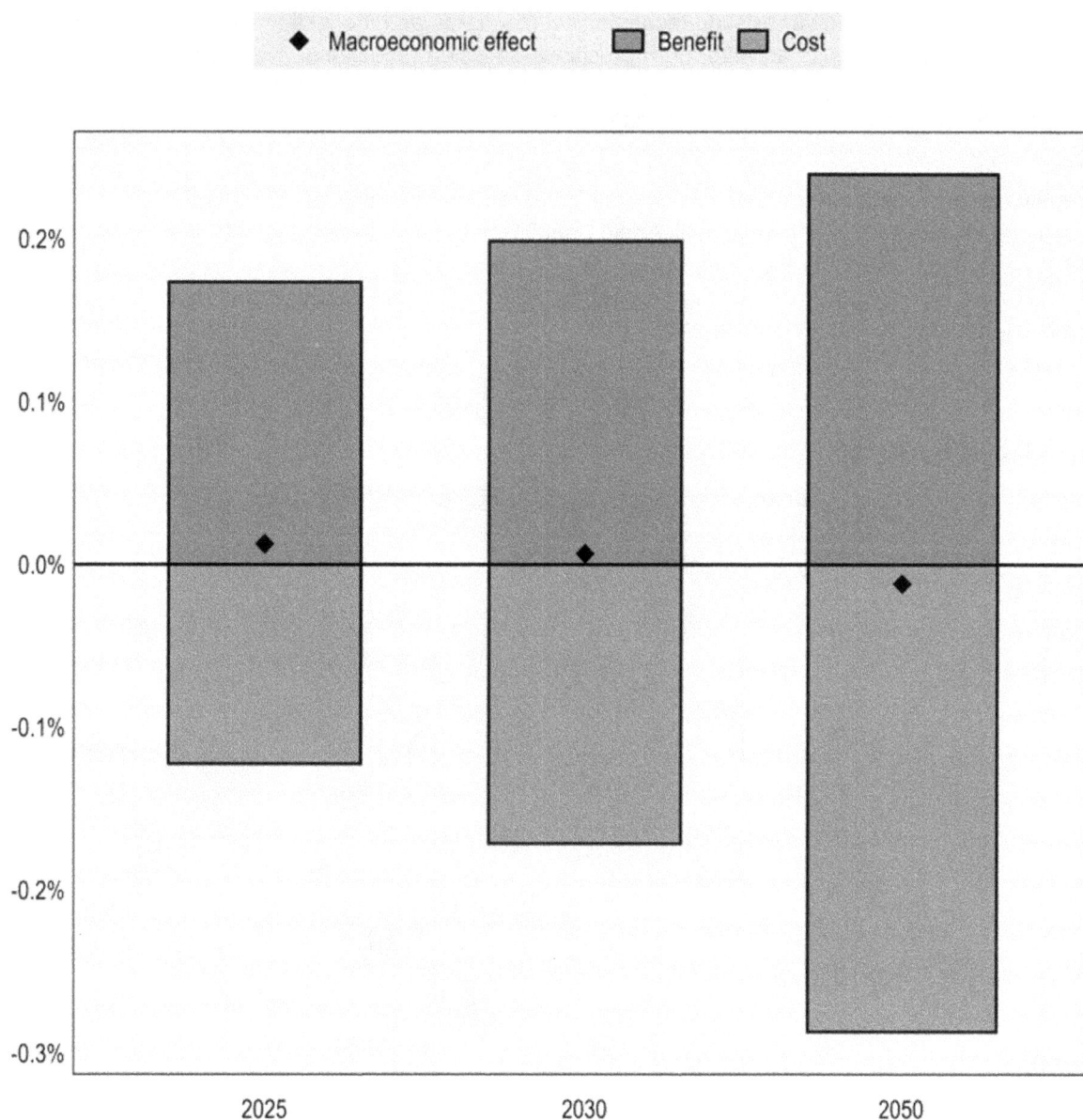

Source: OECD ENV-Linkages model.

StatLink 🖳 https://stat.link/41wq5r

The aggregate results mask differences across countries (Figure 4.2). Whereas all Arctic Council countries benefit economically from reduced air pollution in the MTFR-AC scenario, these benefits are higher in the three largest countries – the United States, Canada, and Russia – than they are in the Nordic countries.[1] Nordic countries are projected to experience smaller changes in emissions between the CLE and MTFR-AC scenarios, as many of the technological improvements have already been implemented in the current legislation scenario.[2] In addition, differences in population density across and within countries further influence the results. In a country like Canada, the population density is drastically different between the north, which has very low population density, and the south, where the largest share of the population lives in urban areas with higher exposure to air pollution. Consequently, as more people benefit from decreased exposure to air pollution, the health and economic benefits are likely to be higher than in other countries.

The costs associated with the BATs deployment also differ by country. Investment costs are particularly high in Russia due to the lower existing technological standards and the less stringent current legislation – this makes it more costly to achieve more ambitious emission reductions. In addition, policy costs are projected to increase substantially in Russia and the Nordic countries by 2050 as their competitiveness declines as they implement stricter regulations than other European countries.

Overall, in the MTFR-AC scenario, the costs resulting from the policy-induced investments in BATs are generally compensated for by the economic benefits of reduced air pollution, making the implementation of such policies close to GDP-neutral in all Arctic Council countries. Specifically, in 2050 the net change in GDP is marginally positive in the United States and Canada, while Nordic countries incur a small GDP loss. In Russia, the net GDP effects of implementing air pollution policies are close to zero but marginally negative, amounting to less than 0.2% of GDP.

Figure 4.2. Regional GDP impact of adopting BATs to reduce air pollution in Arctic Council countries

% GDP, MTFR-AC scenario

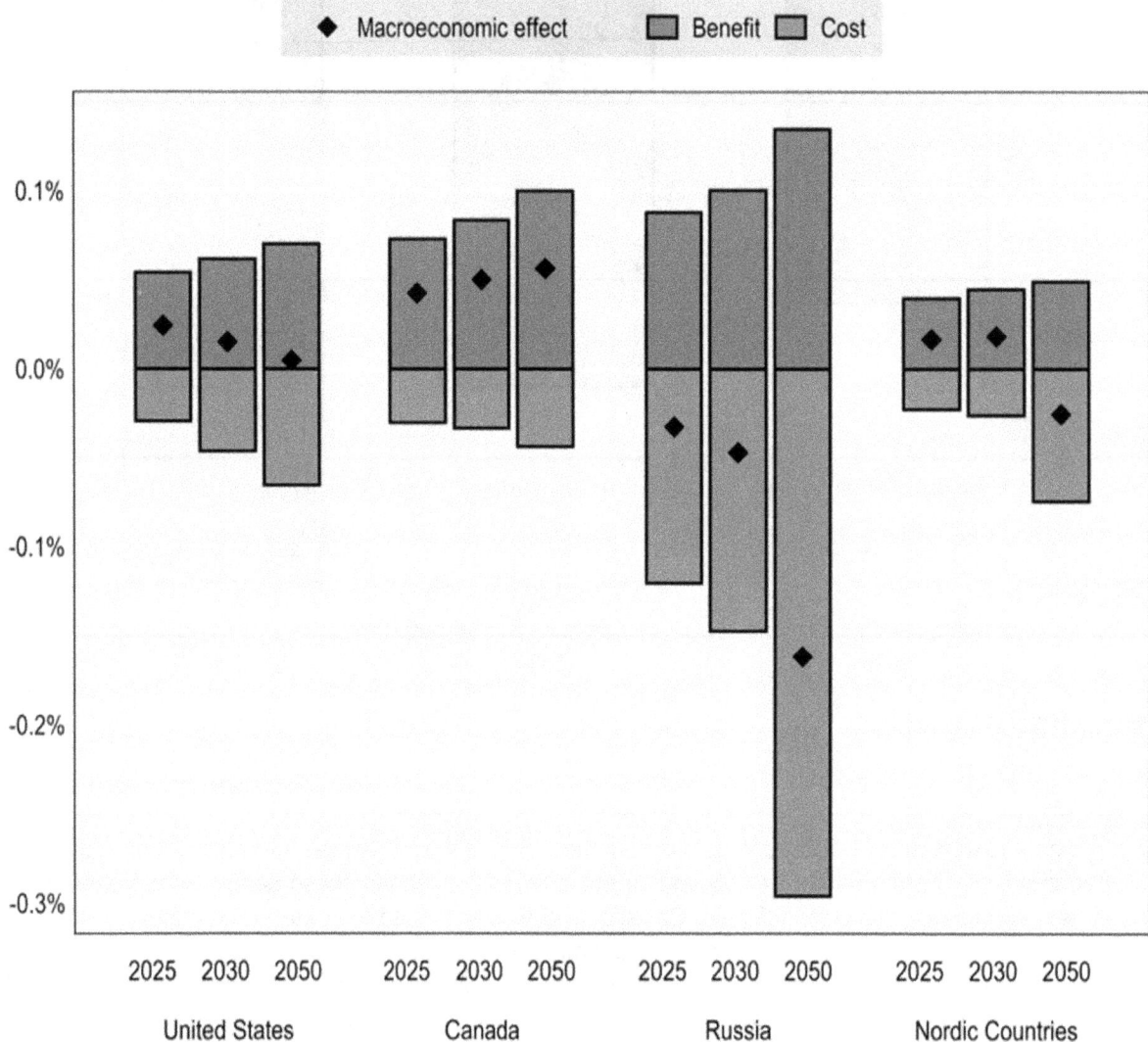

Source: OECD ENV-Linkages model.

StatLink 🔗 https://stat.link/p6d3qs

The size of the benefits, costs and net macroeconomic effects of air pollution policies in Arctic Council countries are small.[3] This is because both policy costs and benefits are the result of adjustments that take place within the economy, as the additional investments and expenditures shift production and trade flows. For example, losses in labour productivity will result in a sectoral loss of output, and if products from these sectors are substituted with imported products; this would imply a loss in competitiveness. On the other hand, investments made in specific sectors comprise an additional sale (e.g. pollution filters), and thus create value added in those sectors.

For these reasons, while the investments needed to deploy BATs in Arctic Council countries imply substantial financial outgoings, the net macroeconomic costs are much lower (Figure 4.3). At the aggregate level in Arctic Council countries, investments in BATs are projected to amount to USD 500 billion in 2050 – i.e. 0.4% of aggregate GDP.[4] Yet the net macroeconomic costs are approximately five times lower, amounting to around USD 100 billion and thus equivalent to 0.07% of the regional GDP. This observation also applies to individual countries that face high costs, such as Russia, where investments in BATs would amount to over 1% of GDP in 2050, but the macroeconomic costs are approximatively equivalent to 0.3% of GDP.

Figure 4.3. Projected investment in BATs versus resulting macroeconomic costs by region

% GDP, MTFR-AC scenario, 2050

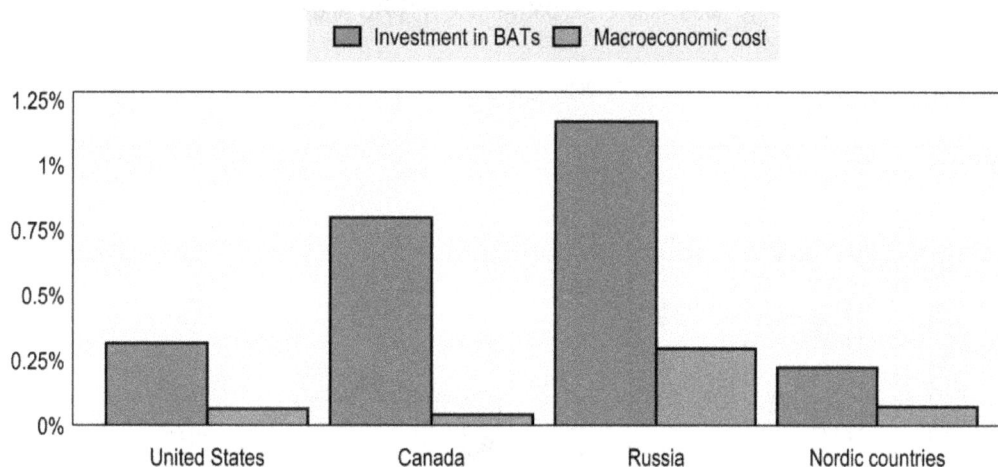

Source: OECD ENV-Linkages model.

StatLink ⟨⟩ https://stat.link/lckn42

4.2. Economic effects of welfare improvements

In addition to the macroeconomic effects presented above, the welfare improvements resulting from air pollution policies also have economic benefits. Welfare improvements result from a reduced risk of mortality and a lower incidence of illness. As outlined in Section 3.3 and Annex B, a variety of valuation techniques can be used to attribute an economic value to mortality and morbidity. The welfare cost of air pollution-related mortality is calculated using the value of a statistical life (VSL; see Box 2.3 in Chapter 2), relying on the OECD methodology to calculate country-specific VSL values (OECD, 2014[1]) as well as the OECD database "Mortality and welfare cost from exposure to environmental risks" (OECD, 2020[2]).

Morbidity impacts are calculated on the basis of previous work by the European Commission on the *Cost-benefit Analysis of Final Policy Scenarios for the EU Clean Air Package* (Holland, 2014[3]).[5]

In the current legislation scenario (CLE), air pollution-related mortality in Arctic Council countries is projected to result in high welfare costs, exceeding USD 750 billion per year by 2050. These costs are projected to occur despite the air quality improvements achieved. While air pollution-related deaths are projected to slightly decrease until 2050, the projected income increases over the period imply a higher VSL, which results in higher welfare costs.

The implementation of additional air pollution policies in Arctic Council countries (MTFR-AC scenario) is projected to result in a significant reduction in the number of deaths, thus translating into welfare improvements. These improvements are projected to already occur in all Arctic Council countries by 2025 and to increase over time in most countries. The countries benefitting the most from these welfare improvements – both in absolute and per capita terms – are Canada, Russia and the United States (Figure 4.4).[6] The main driver of the welfare improvements in these countries is the significant decrease in mortality in the MTFR-AC scenario. Altogether, at the aggregate level, additional air pollution policies are projected to lead to welfare improvements from reduced mortality equivalent to USD 210 billion in 2025, and to reach almost USD 280 billion by 2050.

Figure 4.4. Projected welfare improvements from avoided mortality in Arctic Council countries

USD per capita, 2017 PPP exchange rates, difference between MTFR-AC and CLE scenarios

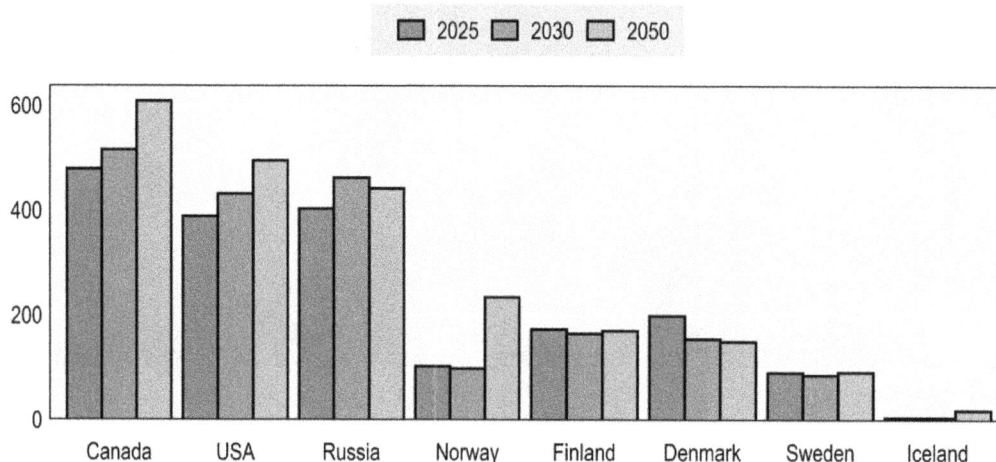

Note: While this report presents a single value estimate for the welfare cost associated with mortality, these values are uncertain. Uncertainty ranges are presented in (OECD, 2016[4]).
Source: (OECD, 2020[2]), *Air Quality and Health: Mortality and welfare cost from exposure to air pollution* (database); Holland (2014[3]), *Cost-benefit Analysis of Final Policy Scenarios for the EU Clean Air Package*; and ENV-Linkages' model projections.

StatLink ⬛ https://stat.link/hordvw

In the MTFR-AC scenario, the reduced incidence of air pollution-related illnesses (morbidity) also generates additional welfare improvements. In all Arctic Council countries, the largest welfare improvements result from a reduced number of days on which normal activities are disrupted (i.e. a lower number of restricted activity days) and from the lower incidence of respiratory diseases, such as asthma and bronchitis (Figure 4.5). At the aggregate level in Arctic Council countries, the yearly welfare improvements associated with reduced morbidity impacts are estimated at USD 12 billion in 2025 and USD 16 billion in 2050. Canada is the country benefitting the most from reduced morbidity, followed by the United States and Russia.

Figure 4.5. Projected welfare improvements from avoided illnesses in Arctic Council countries

USD per capita, 2017 PPP exchange rates, difference between MTFR-AC and CLE scenarios, 2050

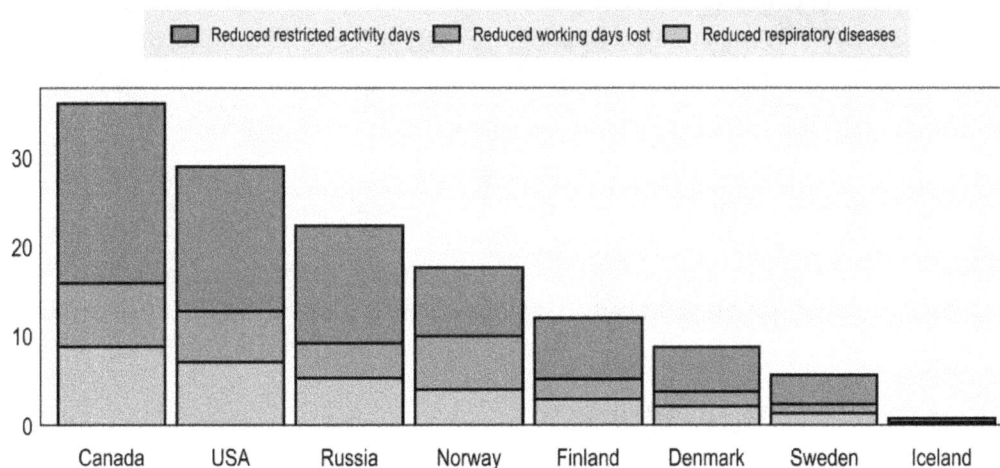

Legend: Reduced restricted activity days | Reduced working days lost | Reduced respiratory diseases

Countries (x-axis): Canada, USA, Russia, Norway, Finland, Denmark, Sweden, Iceland

Note: "Reduced respiratory diseases" includes reduced cases of chronic bronchitis in adults, reduced cases of bronchitis and asthma symptoms in children, and reduced hospital admissions.

Source: (OECD, 2020[2]), *Air Quality and Health: Mortality and welfare cost from exposure to air pollution* (database); Holland (2014[3]), *Cost-benefit Analysis of Final Policy Scenarios for the EU Clean Air Package*; and ENV-Linkages' model projections.

StatLink https://stat.link/0cut4l

While in macroeconomic terms the implementation of additional air pollution policies is likely to be GDP-neutral in the eight Arctic Council countries (Section 4.1), this analysis of welfare effects highlights the large additional benefits of implementing air pollution policies. In summary, this analysis supports the implementation of air pollution policies in Arctic Council countries on the basis of their environmental, health and welfare benefits, which can be achieved without significant impacts on long-run economic growth.

Notes

[1] The results for the Nordic countries are partly driven by the modelling set up. In the ENV-Linkages model, Nordic countries are part of larger aggregate regions also containing European countries that are not part of the Arctic Council (see Table A.2 in Annex A) and that, in the MTFR-AC scenario, do not undertake any new policy action to reduce air pollution. Thus, the aggregate results for this region are likely to be smaller than they would be if the Nordic countries were analysed separately in ENV-Linkages.

[2] For this same reason, any comparison of changes in competitive position among sectors and countries has to be interpreted carefully, as the starting point is not necessarily the same.

[3] This result is similar to the outcome of the analysis of the costs and benefits of air pollution policies in the European Union, performed by the European Commission using the GEM-E3 model (Amann et al., 2017[6]).

[4] All monetary values in this chapter are expressed in 2017 USD PPP.

[5] For details see Annex B.

[6] Per capita costs are calculated using UN population projections (United Nations, 2017[5]).

References

Amann, M. et al. (2017), *Costs, Benefits and Economic Impacts of the EU Clean Air Strategy and their Implications on Innovation and Competitiveness*, International Institute for Applied Systems Analysis (IIASA), Laxenburg. [6]

Holland, M. (2014), *Cost-benefit Analysis of Final Policy Scenarios for the EU Clean Air Package*, Corresponding to IIASA TSAP Report No. 11, International Institute for Applied Systems Analysis (IIASA), Laxenburg, http://ec.europa.eu/environment/air/pdf/TSAP%20CBA.pdf (accessed on 9 March 2021). [3]

OECD (2020), *Air quality and health: Mortality and welfare cost from exposure to air pollution (database)*, Statistics, OECD Environment, https://doi.org/10.1787/c14fb169-en (accessed on 3 November 2020). [2]

OECD (2016), *The Economic Consequences of Outdoor Air Pollution*, OECD Publishing, Paris, https://dx.doi.org/10.1787/9789264257474-en. [4]

OECD (2014), *The Cost of Air Pollution: Health Impacts of Road Transport*, OECD Publishing, Paris, https://dx.doi.org/10.1787/9789264210448-en. [1]

United Nations (2017), *World Population Ageing 2017*, (ST/ESA/SER.A/408), https://population.un.org/ProfilesOfAgeing2017/index.html (accessed on 8 December 2020). [5]

5. Benefits of wider and integrated policy action

As a large share of the air pollutants that reach the Arctic originates from territories outside Arctic Council countries, policy action addressing both long-range pollution and local sources is important to curb pollution. This chapter considers the potential additional benefits for Arctic Council countries of wider geographical adoption of air pollution policies by Arctic Council Observer countries and by the rest of the world. It also models the impacts of global policy action to reduce air pollution alongside climate mitigation and energy transition policies, to highlight the potential additional benefits from such integrated policy action.

5.1. Benefits of wider geographical adoption of air pollution policies

Air quality in Arctic Council countries partly depends on policy action in other regions, as several air pollutants can be transported over long distances. Indeed, limiting transboundary air pollution is recognised as fundamental for reducing air pollution, as stated in the the United Nations Economic Commission for Europe (UNECE) Convention on Long-Range Transboundary Air Pollution (CLRTAP) (UNECE, 2018[1]).

While black carbon emitted closer to the Arctic has a stronger atmospheric warming effect, a greater portion of black carbon particles in the Arctic are emitted from non-Arctic sources (AMAP, 2011[2]), including neighbouring countries, such as Ukraine, China, and many European countries (Sarofim et al., 2009[3]). Black carbon emissions from outside Arctic countries account for two-thirds of black carbon's warming effects in the Arctic (AMAP, 2015[4]). For this reason, policy action addressing both long-range pollution and local sources is important to curb BC pollution in the Arctic.

The implementation of air pollution policies in a wider group of countries would not only be beneficial for the countries implementing the policies, but also for other areas. In order to assess the extent to which Arctic Council countries would benefit from emission reductions taking place in other countries, this section compares the original two scenarios with two new ones: (1) maximum technically feasible reductions implemented in Arctic Council and Observer countries (MTFR-AC&Obs);[1] and (2) MTFR implemented at the global level (MTFR-Global). Comparing these additional scenarios with the scenario previously presented focusing on Arctic Council countries (MTFR-AC) highlights the interactions among the three country groups (i.e. Arctic Council countries, Arctic Council Observer countries, and the rest of the world). Due to data limitations, this chapter focuses solely on the benefits of policy action, without taking into account the costs.[2]

Understanding the impact of wider policy action on air pollution is particularly relevant as many countries outside the Arctic Council show large potential for emission reductions. According to the modelling analysis, the most substantial emission reductions would take place in Observer countries, followed by the rest of the world (see Figure 5.1 for $PM_{2.5}$ projections).

Figure 5.1. Projected global PM$_{2.5}$ concentrations with wider policy action

Annual average anthropogenic PM$_{2.5}$ concentrations, μg/m^3, 2050

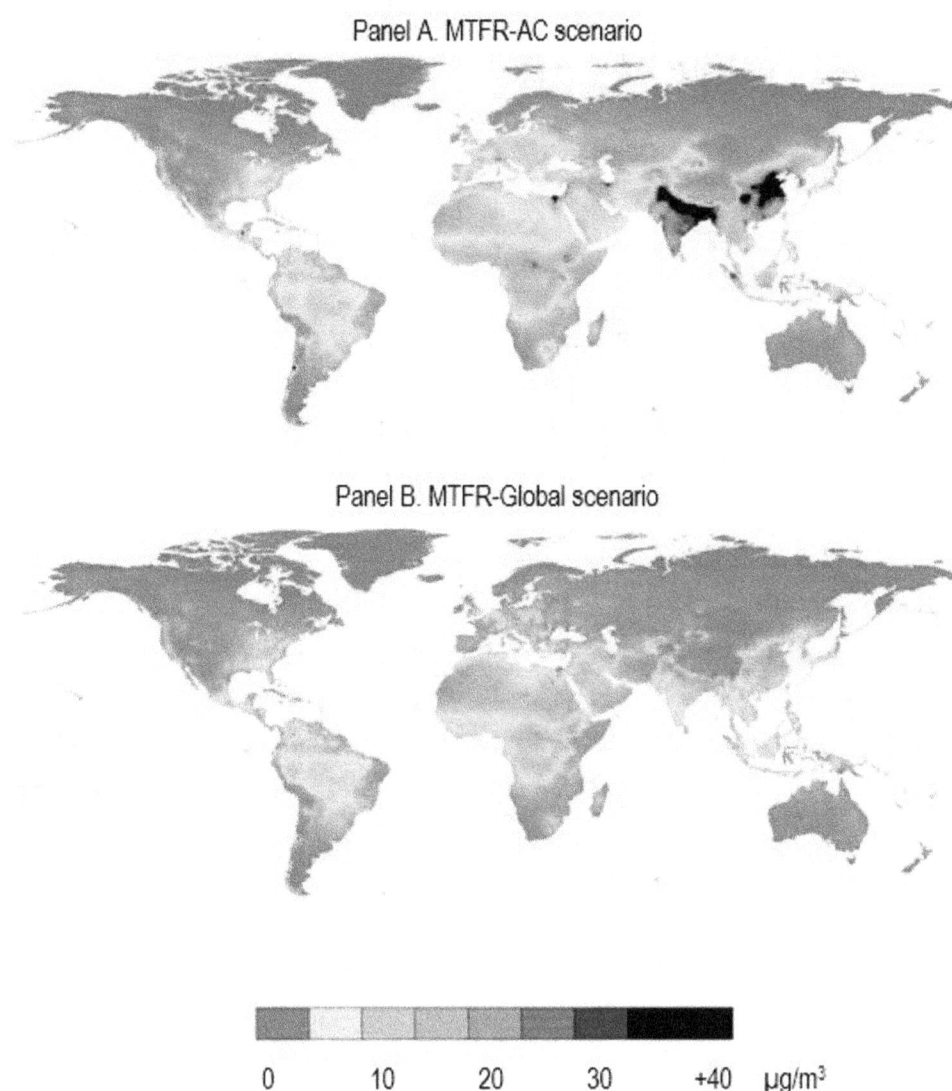

Panel A. MTFR-AC scenario

Panel B. MTFR-Global scenario

| 0 | 10 | 20 | 30 | +40 | μg/m^3 |

Note: μg/m^3: micrograms per cubic metre.
Source: EC-JRC's TM5-FASST model.

Relatively speaking, Arctic Council countries would contribute a smaller share of emission reductions. This is explained by the fact that some large air pollution emitters, such as China and India, are amongst the Observers. Figure 5.2 shows the potential for reductions of PM$_{2.5}$ concentrations in Arctic Council countries when other countries are acting. The comparison of average atmospheric concentrations of PM$_{2.5}$ in Arctic Council countries in the four scenarios highlights the role of transboundary air pollution. For example, PM$_{2.5}$ concentrations in Nordic countries are particularly dependent on emission levels in the Observers, due to Nordic countries' proximity to European Observer countries. Following the same principle, PM$_{2.5}$ concentrations in Russia are at their lowest when MTFR policies are implemented globally, due to the proximity of other Eurasian major emitters. In the United States and Canada, however, PM$_{2.5}$ concentrations are less dependent on emission reductions in neighbouring countries.

Figure 5.2. Projected average $PM_{2.5}$ concentrations in Arctic Council countries with wider policy action

Annual average population-weighted anthropogenic $PM_{2.5}$ concentrations, $\mu g/m^3$, 2050

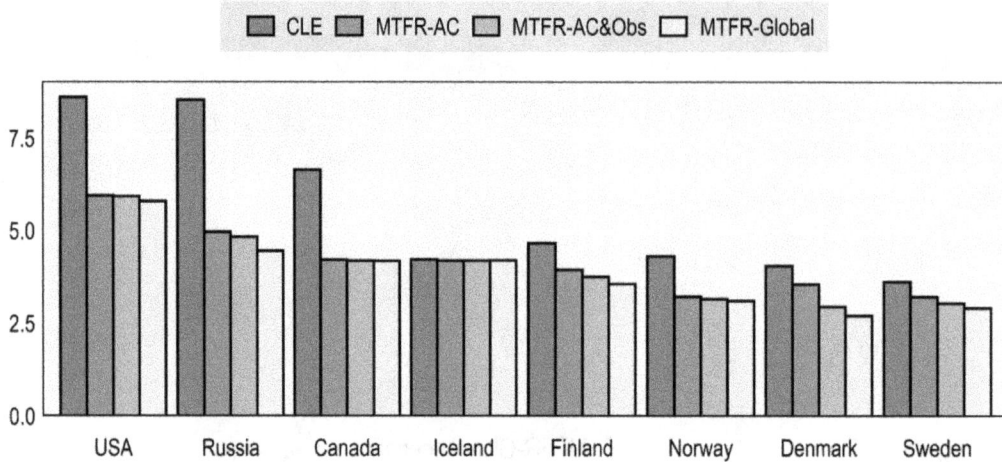

Note: $\mu g/m^3$: micrograms per cubic metre.
Source: EC-JRC's TM5-FASST model.

StatLink ᴍɪ🔊 https://stat.link/qzk4sw

By 2050, the global implementation of the MTFR scenario (MTFR-Global) would save 20% more lives in Arctic Council countries than the MTFR-AC scenario, implying 100 000 fewer air pollution-related deaths a year than in the CLE scenario (Figure 5.3). Nevertheless, the largest mortality reductions in Arctic Council countries are attributed to air quality improvements from domestic policy action, amounting to around 80 000 fewer deaths.

Similarly, mortality reductions are attributed to air quality improvements within the region also in the other two country groups (Observers and rest of the world). Hence, by reducing their pollutant emissions, every country would also benefit from improved human and environmental health domestically, as displayed in Figure 5.3.

Figure 5.3. Projected impact of wider policy action on air pollution-related mortality

Thousands deaths per year, 2050

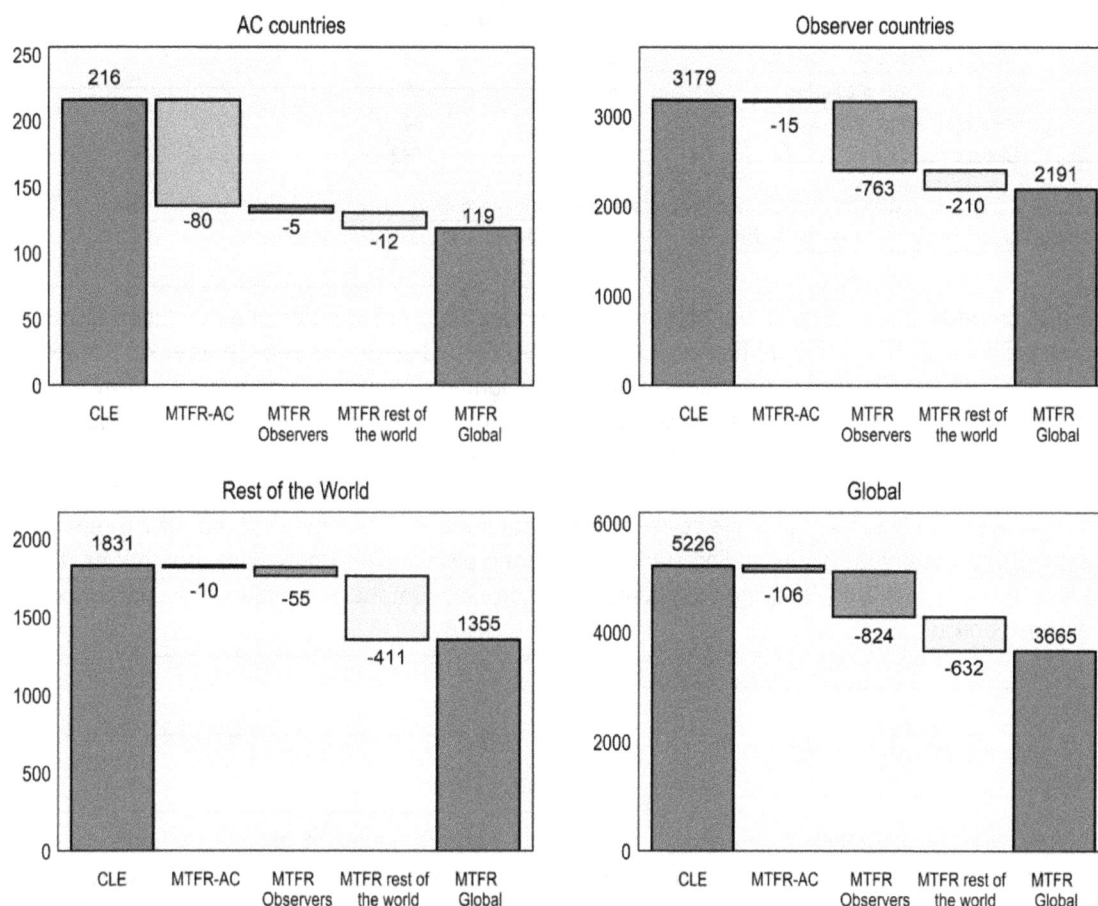

Notes: Each graph shows the number of deaths in that region projected from the different levels of geographical coverage of the MTFR policy. Each graph shows the potential additional contribution of each country group to reducing mortality. The bar on the left shows the initial values from the baseline (CLE) scenario, from which the contribution of each scenario is subtracted, to arrive at the total (MTFR-Global). The graphs relate to premature deaths due to fine particles as well as ground-level ozone.
Source: ENV-Linkages' model projections, based on Global Burden of Disease (GBD, 2018[5]).

StatLink 🔢📊 https://stat.link/sx7q3u

The reduction in mortality translates into significant welfare improvements. By 2050, compared to action by Arctic Council countries alone, when Arctic Council Observers also implement air pollution policies, welfare improvements in Arctic Council countries would amount to USD 15 billion more per year. There would be an additional USD 56 billion in welfare benefits in Arctic Council countries if all countries were to implement MTFR policies, bringing the total to USD 339 billion (Table 5.1). The implementation of MTFR policies in Arctic Council and Observer countries would improve global welfare by almost USD 2 trillion every year by the middle of the century compared to the continuation of current policies, with 15% of this total welfare improvement taking place in Arctic Council countries. In the MTFR-Global scenario, global annual welfare improvements would be even higher, reaching over USD 3 trillion by 2050 (Table 5.1).

Table 5.1. Projected welfare improvements by region with wider policy action

Comparison with the CLE scenario, annual impact, billion USD 2017 PPP, 2050

	MTFR – AC	MTFR – AC & Obs	MTFR - Global
Impacts in Arctic Council countries	283	298	339
Impacts in Observer countries	38	1 662	2 079
Impacts in the rest of the world	20	94	730
Global impacts	341	2 042	3 148

Source: (OECD, 2020[6]), *Air Quality and Health: Mortality and welfare cost from exposure to air pollution* (database); (Holland, 2014[7]), *Cost-benefit Analysis of Final Policy Scenarios for the EU Clean Air Package*; and ENV-Linkages' model projections.

There would be additional economic benefits from the reduced market impacts of air pollution (for impacts on sectoral productivity and consumption choices in the MTFR-AC scenario; see Chapter 4). For example, as $PM_{2.5}$ emissions are reduced in a broader number of countries, the resulting health and environmental improvements lead to lower market costs of air pollution in most countries and regions, eventually resulting in higher economic growth. However, the necessary investments in BATs are likely to be particularly large for countries with high levels of air pollution or laxer air pollution policies. Overall, a wider implementation of MTFR policies is likely to have positive consequences for the competitiveness of manufacturers in Arctic Council countries. As industries in trading partner countries also implement similar regulations, they are likely to face similar costs, thus levelling the playing field across countries and making it easier for countries to tighten their policies.

5.2. Benefits of integrating air pollution, climate mitigation and energy transition policies

Air pollution, climate mitigation and energy policies are strongly linked due to significant overlaps in emission sources and policy solutions. Thus, addressing key emitting sectors, such as transport and fossil-fuel based power generation, can achieve joint benefits for tackling both air pollution and climate change (Lanzi and Dellink, 2019[8]). Air pollution policies can lead to structural change in the economy, specifically driving a shift in production towards cleaner sectors; this would also lower greenhouse gas emissions. Similarly, climate mitigation and energy policies can reduce air pollution. For example, reducing fossil fuel combustion is normally beneficial for both climate mitigation and air quality, except when fossil fuel is substituted with biomass combustion for residential heating, which increases emissions of combustion-related air pollutants, such as black carbon.

In order to assess the interactions among air pollution, climate mitigation and energy transition policies, this section considers a scenario that includes the global coverage of the MTFR scenario (MTFR-Global) together with the implementation of the Sustainable Development Scenario (SDS) developed by the International Energy Agency (IEA) for the World Energy Outlook (IEA, 2018[9]). This scenario (MTFR-SDS) represents a more stringent policy mix that targets air pollution while also implementing climate mitigation policies and a transition to a cleaner energy system (IEA, 2018[9]). The modelling analysis explores the potential environmental, health and welfare benefits of this integrated policy action. Due to data limitations, however, the analysis does not take into account the costs of policy action.

In the MTFR-SDS scenario, countries would see air pollution fall even more substantially than under the MTFR-Global scenario alone. This is the case for Arctic Council countries (Panel A, Figure 5.4), as well as across the globe (Panel B, Figure 5.4). At the same time, the MTFR-SDS scenario has the potential to slow down global warming. Greenhouse gas emissions are already projected to decline in the MTFR-Global scenario, as illustrated for carbon dioxide (CO_2), nitrous oxide (N_2O), and methane (CH_4). This highlights the potential for air pollution policies to also contribute to mitigating climate change.

However, the MTFR-SDS scenario involves greater curbs on GHG emissions– both in Arctic Council countries and at the global level – through climate mitigation and energy policies.

Figure 5.4. Projected air pollution and greenhouse gas emission reductions from integrated policy action

Indexed, CLE = 1, 2050

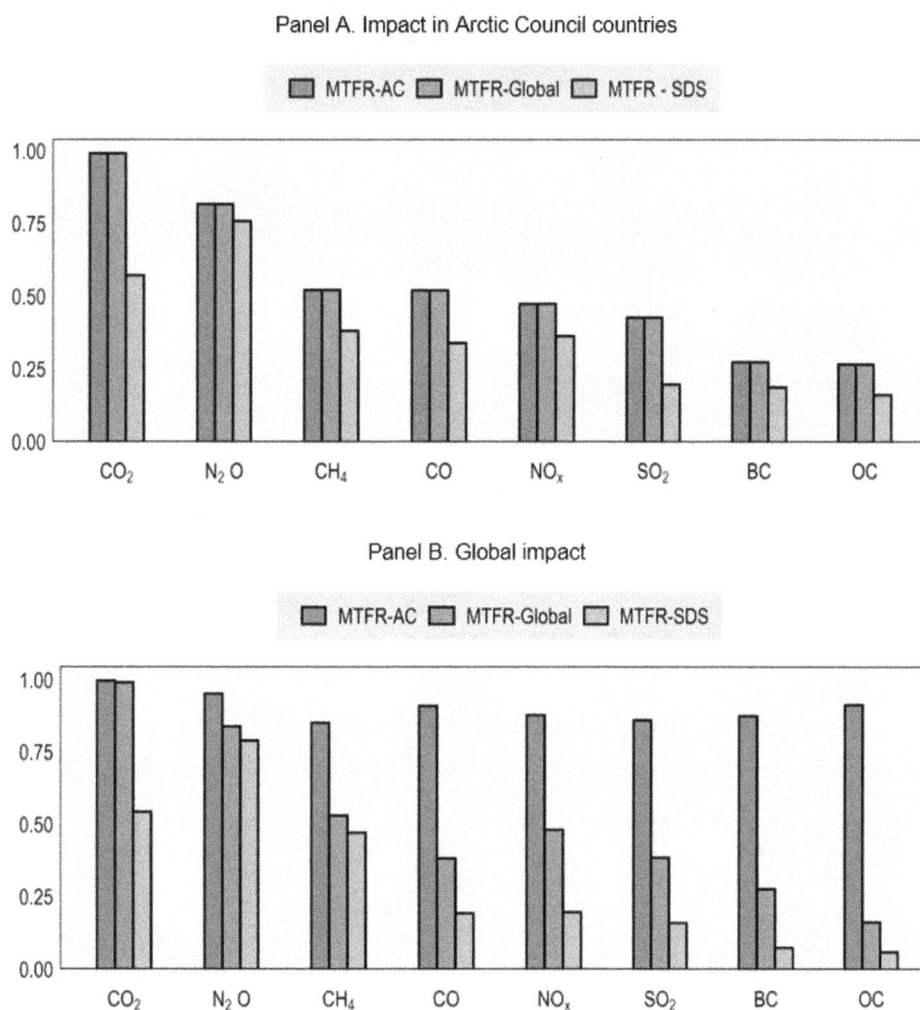

Panel A. Impact in Arctic Council countries

Panel B. Global impact

Source: ENV-Linkages, based on input from IIASA's GAINS model.

StatLink https://stat.link/7w5f2p

When looking at specific GHGs, methane is the greenhouse gas that shows the strongest interactions with air pollution policies. Indeed, methane emissions are nearly halved when the best available techniques of the MTFR scenario are deployed at the global level (MTFR-Global) (Höglund-Isaksson et al., 2020[10]). The MTFR-SDS scenario leads to further methane emission reductions. These synergetic effects in the reduction of air pollutants and methane emissions are important, especially given the high radiative forcing of methane, which on a 100-year timeframe has a warming potential 28 times higher than that of CO_2, as estimated in the Fifth IPCC Assessment Report (IPCC, 2013[11]). These changes in methane emissions refer exclusively to anthropogenic sources. Natural sources of methane, such as oceans and soils in permafrost regions, are not accounted for in this analysis, as they result from natural processes. Nonetheless, even natural releases of methane can be exacerbated by global warming. Thus, reducing the emissions of greenhouse gas and short-lived climate pollutants, such as black carbon, would also generate additional co-benefits in and beyond the Arctic, by reducing the risk of natural methane releases.

Besides significant climate co-benefits, the implementation of more stringent policies under the MTFR-SDS scenario would also reduce mortality associated with exposure to PM$_{2.5}$ and ground-level ozone. Overall, by 2050 in the MTFR-SDS scenario, air pollution-related deaths in Arctic Council countries would be half the level of the baseline scenario (CLE) (Figure 5.5, Panel A). Globally by 2050, the MTFR-SDS scenario could avoid half a million more deaths than the MTFR-Global scenario (Figure 5.5, Panel B).

Figure 5.5. Projected impact of integrated policy action on air pollution-related mortality

2050

Panel A. Arctic Council countries (Thousand deaths per year)

Panel B. Global (Million deaths per year)

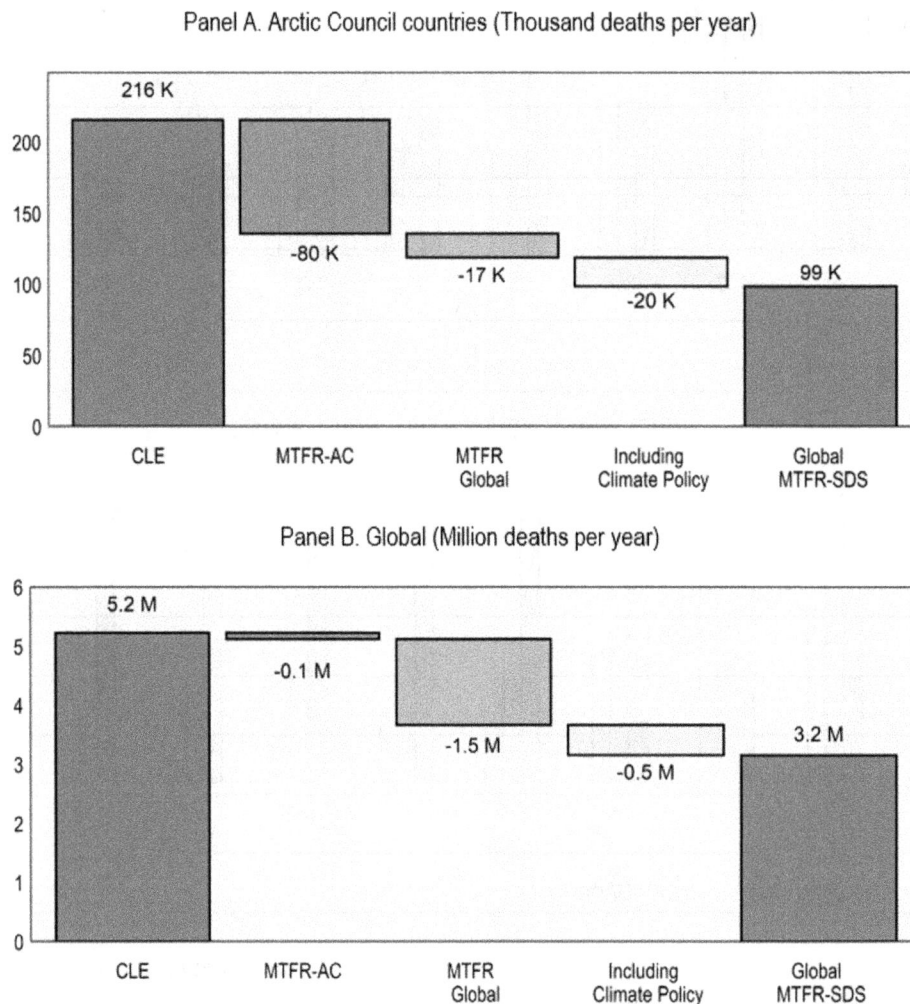

Notes: The two graphs use different scales (Thousand in Panel A and Million in Panel B). Each graph shows the number of deaths in that region projected from the different levels of policy ambition. Each graph shows the potential additional contribution of the different levels of policy ambition to reducing mortality. The bar on the left shows the initial values from the baseline (CLE) scenario, from which the contribution of each scenario is subtracted, to arrive at the total (Global MTFR-SDS). The graphs relate to premature deaths due to fine particles as well as ground-level ozone.

Source: ENV-Linkages' model projections, based on Global Burden of Disease (GBD, 2018[5]).

StatLink 🔗 https://stat.link/2741bq

The positive environmental and health outcomes stemming from the MTFR-SDS scenario are likely to translate into welfare improvements, which in comparison to the MTFR-Global scenario, would amount to almost USD 70 billion more in 2050 Arctic Council countries. (Table 5.2). At the global level, compared to the MTFR-Global scenario, the MTFR-SDS scenario would add at least another USD 1 trillion in global welfare benefits by 2050, with 10% of these welfare improvements taking place in Arctic Council countries.

While these estimates only account for welfare improvements from reduced air pollution-related mortality, the mitigating impact on climate change of lower GHG emissions would lead to additional welfare benefits, most notably those resulting from reduced mortality from air-borne diseases, temperature extremes, and climate disasters.

Table 5.2. Projected welfare improvements by region with integrated policy action

Comparison with the CLE scenario, annual impact, billion USD 2017 PPP, 2050

	MTFR - AC	MTFR - Global	MTFR – SDS
Impacts in Arctic Council	283	339	408
Impacts in Observer countries	38	2 079	2 745
Impacts in rest of the world	20	730	1 003
Global impacts	341	3 148	4 146

Source: ENV-Linkages' model projections, based on OECD VLS values from the OECD Environment Database (OECD, 2020[6]); and morbidity values from Holland (2014[7]).

Additional policy action to reduce greenhouse gas emissions is also likely to result in economic benefits from the reduced air pollution impacts. However, as the policy costs of implementing the MTFR-SDS scenario are also likely to be higher, the net macroeconomic effects are difficult to predict.[3]

Finally, reducing GHG emissions through air pollution, climate mitigation and energy policies would also lead to additional benefits resulting from reduced climate risks and impacts (OECD, 2015[12]). Mitigating climate change at the global level would be particularly beneficial for the Arctic region and its ecosystems. Indeed, the effects of climate change on the Arctic environment – which include a reduction of sea-ice and permafrost, changes in weather and temperatuare patterns, severe loss of biodiversity and ecosystem services, and damages to indigenous communities – are becoming increasingly visible. In turn, Arctic warming has severe repercussions at the global level, causing rising sea levels, changes in climate and precipitation patterns, increasing frequency of severe weather events, and loss of fish stocks, among other risks. Therefore, when considering all the regional and global consequences of climate change, the benefits of policy action highlighted in this section are likely to be underestimated.

Notes

[1] This scenario expands policy action to Arctic Council Observer countries, which include China France, Germany, India, Italy, Japan, Korea, the Netherlands, Poland, Singapore, Spain, Switzerland, and the United Kingdom. Observer countries can participate in meetings and areas of work of the Arctic Council. Decisions within the Arctic Council can only be made by the eight Arctic Council countries (Arctic Council, 2019[13]).

[2] The main reason for this is that detailed regional costs are not available at the global level. In any case, the main analysis is focused on Arctic Council countries, for which estimates of both costs and benefits are calculated.

[3] A full assessment of the macroeconomic effects of the MTFR-SDS scenario at the global level is beyond the scope of this report.

References

AMAP (2015), *Summary for Policy-makers: Arctic Climate Issues 2015*, Arctic Monitoring and Assessment Programme (AMAP), Oslo, https://www.amap.no/documents/doc/summary-for-policy-makers-arctic-climate-issues-2015/1196 (accessed on 4 December 2020). [4]

AMAP (2011), *The Impact of Black Carbon on Arctic Climate*, Arctic Monitoring and Assessment Programme (AMAP), Oslo, https://www.amap.no/documents/doc/the-impact-of-black-carbon-on-arctic-climate/746. [2]

Arctic Council (2019), *Arctic Council Observer Manual for Subsidiary Bodies*, Arctic Council, http://hdl.handle.net/11374/939 (accessed on 10 March 2021). [13]

GBD (2018), "Global Burden of Disease Study 2017: All cause Mortality and Life Expectancy 1950-2017, Global Burden of Disease Collaborative Network.", *Seattle, United States: Institute for Health Metrics and Evaluation (IHME)*. [5]

Höglund-Isaksson, L. et al. (2020), "Technical potentials and costs for reducing global anthropogenic methane emissions in the 2050 timeframe –results from the GAINS model", *Environmental Research Communications*, Vol. 2/2, p. 025004, http://dx.doi.org/10.1088/2515-7620/ab7457. [10]

Holland, M. (2014), *Cost-benefit Analysis of Final Policy Scenarios for the EU Clean Air Package*, Corresponding to IIASA TSAP Report No. 11, International Institute for Applied Systems Analysis (IIASA), Laxenburg, http://ec.europa.eu/environment/air/pdf/TSAP%20CBA.pdf (accessed on 9 March 2021). [7]

IEA (2018), *World Energy Outlook 2018*, International Energy Agency, Paris, https://dx.doi.org/10.1787/weo-2018-en. [9]

IPCC (2013), *The Physical Science Basis. Contribution of Working Group I to the Fifth Assessment Report of the Intergovernmental Panel on Climate Change*, Cambridge University Press, Cambridge, United Kingdom and New York, NY, USA, https://www.ipcc.ch/report/ar5/wg1/. [11]

Lanzi, E. and A. Dellink (2019), *Economic interactions between climate change and outdoor air pollution*, OECD Environment Working Papers, No. 148, OECD Publishing, Paris, https://doi.org/10.1787/8e4278a2-en. [8]

OECD (2020), *Air quality and health: Mortality and welfare cost from exposure to air pollution (database)*, Statistics, OECD Environment, https://doi.org/10.1787/c14fb169-en (accessed on 3 November 2020). [6]

OECD (2015), *The Economic Consequences of Climate Change*, OECD Publishing, Paris, https://dx.doi.org/10.1787/9789264235410-en. [12]

Sarofim, M. et al. (2009), *Current Policies, Emission Trends and Mitigation Options for Black Carbon in the Arctic Region*, https://iiasa.ac.at/rains/reports/DRAFTWhitePaper-BCArcticMitigation-280909.pdf. [3]

UNECE (2018), *Decision 2018/5 Long-term strategy for the Convention on Long-range Transboundary Air Pollution for 2020−2030 and beyond*, https://unece.org/fileadmin/DAM/env/documents/2018/Air/EB/correct_numbering_Decision_2 018_5.pdf (accessed on 10 March 2021). [1]

6. Overall benefits of air pollution policies

This final chapter first briefly summarises the benefits of air pollution policies quantified in the modelling analysis and outlined in previous chapters. The chapter then highlights the additional benefits from reducing air pollution that could not be accounted for in the quantitative scenario analysis. It includes an overview of the climate benefits from reduced emissions of short-lived climate pollutants. These additional benefits strengthen the call for policy action on air pollution.

6.1. Benefits of air pollution policies quantified in the modelling analysis

The quantitative scenario analysis presented in previous chapters of this report has highlighted the potential environmental, health and economic benefits of policy action to improve air quality in Arctic Council countries.

More ambitious air pollution policies are projected to result in emission reductions that lead to substantial air quality improvements. With lower exposure to air pollution, air pollution-related health impacts would also decrease. In particular, air pollution-related deaths would decrease. While the net macroeconomic effects are close to zero, the welfare improvements from reduced mortality and morbidity are high.

Inevitably, the results in the modelling analysis are subject to uncertainties concerning the economic projections, the estimations of emission projections and of concentrations of air pollution, the quantification of the biophysical impacts of air pollution, and the evaluation of the economic consequences. While changes to the modelling framework and key parameters would lead to changes in the numerical results, they would not affect the overall conclusions and policy messages that show the beneficial effects of air pollution policies (OECD, 2016[1]).

6.2. Additional benefits of air pollution policies

There are many additional benefits from reducing air pollution that could not be included in the analysis due to lack of data. These add to the rationale for policy action on air pollution. For example, besides the numerous health impacts of $PM_{2.5}$ and ground-level ozone discussed in this report, air pollution can also have other impacts on health, affecting fertility (Nieuwenhuijsen et al., 2014[2]), cognitive abilities in children (Sunyer et al., 2015[3]; Allen et al., 2017[4]; Basner et al., 2014[5]) and low weight at birth (Wang et al., 1997[6]). The latter two impacts are particularly important as they can have long-term effects on children's school outcomes (Zhang, Chen and Zhang, 2018[7]), education levels and therefore earnings, with long-term implications for human capital.

Additionally, SO_2 and NO_x have direct impacts on health, leading to respiratory symptoms such as increased bronchitis symptoms in children with asthma (WHO, 2013[8]; Walton et al., 2015[9]), as well as increased mortality (RCP, 2016[10]).

Similarly, the use of fertilisers in agriculture leads to negative local environmental impacts, including water and soil pollution. Reducing fertilisers would imply healthier ecosystems, greater food quality and lower health risks.

Additional health benefits can occur specifically in urban areas when traffic circulation is limited to tackle air pollution emissions. These include reduced noise and traffic congestion, which can both affect health. Transport-related air pollution policies can also encourage people to be more active, with further potential health benefits (OECD, 2019[11]).

Finally, exposure to air pollution can also exacerbate the consequences of diseases that affect the respiratory system, such as COVID-19 (Wu et al., 2020[12]). Health damage resulting from long-term exposure to air pollution can diminish the body's ability to fend off respiratory infections. Research found that a person living for decades in areas in the US with high levels of fine particulate matter is 15% more likely to die from COVID-19 than someone in a region with one unit less of the fine particulate pollution (Wu et al., 2020[12]).

There are also additional economic benefits from better air quality beyond those from improved health and agricultural productivity. High concentrations of air pollution can damage buildings and cultural heritage (Screpanti and De Marco, 2009[13]), decrease visibility, and reduce tourism (Dong, Xu and Wong, 2019[14]). Furthermore, air pollution can have negative impacts on biodiversity, forests and ecosystems (UNEP,

2010[15]). These impacts are likely to generate significant value losses, additional expenditures and an overall disutility, affecting human activity and economy.

Finally, while this report focuses on the macroeconomic effects and welfare improvements, improved air quality can also have beneficial effects on well-being. A recent OECD report highlights the potential benefits of environmental policies on well-being, including quality of life improvements from improved air quality (OECD, 2019[11]).

6.3. Climate benefits from reducing emissions of short-lived climate pollutants

Short-lived climate pollutants (SLCPs) have a warming impact on the climate and include black carbon, methane, ground-level ozone, and hydrofluorocarbons. Reducing SLCP emissions could help preserve the local Arctic climate and prevent some global impacts of climate change, including a rise in sea levels, changes in weather patterns, and loss of fish stocks.[1] Although these climate benefits are not included in this report, they add weight to the economic case for increased policy action on air pollution, including SLCPs, in Arctic Council countries.

According to O'Garra (2017[16]), Arctic ecosystems provide value to society equivalent to about USD 287 billion per year[2] in food supply, mineral extraction, oil production, tourism and leisure, as well as climate regulation services. Many of these services could be lost due to a rapidly changing climate. For example, changes to the local Arctic climate can have severe repercussions for Arctic wildlife and communities, which are highly dependent on natural resources. The thinning of sea ice and the lengthening melt season have made it hard for Northern local communities to obtain wild sources of food.

Reducing SLCP emissions, and the resulting climate impacts, could mitigate the potential release and transport of persistent organic pollutants (POPs), such as organochlorine pesticides, industrial chemicals and dioxins, and mercury, to the Arctic environment. Rising temperatures could result in the release of deposits of POPs and increase the potential for the long-range transport of POPs in gaseous form or alongside aerosol particles such as black carbon (Ma, Hung and Macdonald, 2016[17]). Two recent reports from the Arctic Monitoring and Assessment Programme (AMAP) show the negative impact of POPs on the Arctic environment (AMAP, 2016[18]; Science for Environment Policy, 2017[19]; AMAP/UN Environment, 2019[20]). These include high dietary exposure to mercury and other POPs through the accumulation of these two elements in fresh water fish and large mammals. These especially affect the Arctic's indigenous population, who consume these animals more than people in urban areas. Despite decreasing in previous decades, the levels of POPs in indigenous people's blood are still high enough to cause neurological and cardiovascular damage (AMAP, 2016[21]).

Thawing permafrost can lead to releases of carbon dioxide and methane that would aggravate climate change and result in high economic costs (Hope and Schaefer, 2015[22]). There are a large number of natural methane and organic carbon deposits in the Arctic, on the seabed, and in soils and lake sediments. The contribution of short-lived climate pollutants to climate change can create conditions suitable for the decomposition of the organic material in these reservoirs, which can release methane, with further warming effects on the climate (AMAP, 2015[23]).

Slowing down global warming in Arctic Council countries might also limit climate impacts that would otherwise lead to increases in specific emission sources. For example, climate change can result in increased incidence of forest fires, due to ice and snow melting and higher temperatures (Kim et al., 2020[24]). Similarly, as Arctic sea ice recedes, shipping activities might also increase (ITF, 2018[25]; AMAP, 2015[26]), resulting in higher emissions. In turn, forest fires and shipping contribute to air pollution and short-lived climate pollutants emissions, thus leading to a vicious cycle that aggravates the climate crisis.

Finally, the Arctic hosts multiple climate tipping points[3] that could be triggered by changes in the local climate. The Arctic sea-ice loss amplifies global warming caused by the surface albedo impacts (Yumashev et al., 2019[27]) and the Greenland Ice Sheet disintegration may lead to global sea level rise of up to 7 metres (Dowdeswell, 2006[28]). These ice-loss events could trigger other climate tipping points, such as the slowdown of the Atlantic Meridional Overturning Circulation (AMOC) that could change weather patterns in Europe (Jackson et al., 2015[29]) and permafrost thawing that could release large amounts of carbon dioxide and natural methane deposits, further enhancing global warming (AMAP, 2015[23]; Gasser et al., 2018[30]).

6.4. A call for policy action on air pollution

To conclude, despite uncertainties about the exact figures presented in this report, there are clear environmental, health and welfare benefits in scaling up commitments to reduce air pollution in Arctic Council countries. Furthermore, climate change and socio-economic developments might exacerbate future environmental impacts of air pollution. This risk should encourage countries to put in place policy action to reduce air pollution.

Policy action on air pollution requires an all-encompassing approach that considers all emission sources. Policy options include incentivising or requiring the adoption of cleaner technologies, implementing air quality standards, automobile emission standards, fuel quality standards, and emission taxes, among others. Urban policies leading to reduced traffic would also imply lower non-exhaust emissions from cars (OECD, 2020[31]).

Policy action on air pollution can also benefit from interactions with other policy domains. Reducing air pollution though the deployment of the best available techniques provides an opportunity to reap synergies with investments in green growth and promoting innovation. As highlighted in Chapter 5 and Section 6.3, there are strong interactions between air pollution and climate change (Lanzi and Dellink, 2019[32]). Integrated policies that consider trade-offs and co-benefits for policy objectives on climate change, energy and air pollution are needed. Stimulating energy efficiency is the typical example of an integrated policy response that has multiple benefits (IEA, 2014[33]).

While this report focuses specifically on Arctic Council countries and their key role in contributing to preserving the Arctic environment, additional policy action on air pollution will be beneficial to most countries and could contribute to slowing down global warming through a substantial reduction of short-lived climate pollutants.

The current momentum for building back better after the COVD-19 pandemic and for a low-carbon transition creates opportunities for governments to also improve air quality, health and make progress towards sustainable development goals. Leveraging this momentum will help to establish a more central role for air quality policies, which can contribute to improving both human health and the environment.

Notes

[1] See for example results on historical ocean's warming on marine fisheries production (Free et al., 2019[35])

[2] The original figure reported in O'Garra (2017[16]) is USD 281 billion per year (in 2016 USD PPP). It has been converted to 2017 USD PPP for comparability with other estimates in this report.

[3] The IPCC defines a tipping point as a critical threshold at which global or regional climate changes from one stable state to another stable state, usually in a non-linear and often irreversible way (IPCC, 2019[34]).

References

Allen, J. et al. (2017), "Cognitive Effects of Air Pollution Exposures and Potential Mechanistic Underpinnings", *Current Environmental Health Reports*, Vol. 4/2, pp. 180-191, http://dx.doi.org/10.1007/s40572-017-0134-3. [4]

AMAP (2016), *AMAP Assessment 2015: Human Health in the Arctic*, https://www.amap.no/documents/doc/amap-assessment-2015-human-health-in-the-arctic/1346. [21]

AMAP (2016), *AMAP Assessment 2015: Temporal Trends in Persistent Organic Pollutants in the Arctic. Arctic Monitoring and Assessment Programme (AMAP)*, https://www.amap.no/documents/doc/amap-assessment-2015-temporal-trends-in-persistent-organic-pollutants-in-the-arctic/1521. [18]

AMAP (2015), *Arctic Monitoring and Assessment Programme (AMAP) AMAP Assessment 2015: Methane as an Arctic climate forcer*, https://www.amap.no/documents/download/2499/inline (accessed on 12 March 2021). [23]

AMAP (2015), *Summary for Policy-makers: Arctic Climate Issues 2015*, http://www.amap.no/documents/18/documents/2 (accessed on 26 April 2019). [26]

AMAP/UN Environment (2019), *Technical Background Report for the Global Mercury Assessment 2018*. [20]

Basner, M. et al. (2014), "Auditory and non-auditory effects of noise on health", *The Lancet*, Vol. 383/9925, pp. 1325-1332, http://dx.doi.org/10.1016/s0140-6736(13)61613-x. [5]

Dong, D., X. Xu and Y. Wong (2019), "Estimating the Impact of Air Pollution on Inbound Tourism in China: An Analysis Based on Regression Discontinuity Design", *Sustainability*, Vol. 11/6, p. 1682, http://dx.doi.org/10.3390/su11061682. [14]

Dowdeswell, J. (2006), "ATMOSPHERIC SCIENCE: The Greenland Ice Sheet and Global Sea-Level Rise", *Science*, Vol. 311/5763, pp. 963-964, http://dx.doi.org/10.1126/science.1124190. [28]

Free, C. et al. (2019), "Impacts of historical warming on marine fisheries production", *Science*, pp. 979-983, http://dx.doi.org/10.1126/science.aau1758. [35]

Gasser, T. et al. (2018), "Path-dependent reductions in CO2 emission budgets caused by permafrost carbon release", *Nature Geoscience*, Vol. 11/11, pp. 830-835, http://dx.doi.org/10.1038/s41561-018-0227-0. [30]

Hope, C. and K. Schaefer (2015), "Economic impacts of carbon dioxide and methane released from thawing permafrost", *Nature Climate Change*, Vol. 6/1, pp. 56-59, http://dx.doi.org/10.1038/nclimate2807. [22]

IEA (2014), *Capturing the Multiple Benefits of Energy Efficiency: A Guide to Quantifying the Value Added*, International Energy Agency, Paris, https://dx.doi.org/10.1787/9789264220720-en. [33]

IPCC (2019), *Special Report on the Ocean and Cryosphere in a Changing Climate*. [34]

ITF (2018), *Decarbonising Maritime Transport: Pathways to Zero-carbon Shipping by 2035*, OECD Publishing, Paris, https://www.oecd-ilibrary.org/transport/decarbonising-maritime-transport_b1a7632c-en. [25]

Jackson, L. et al. (2015), "Global and European climate impacts of a slowdown of the AMOC in a high resolution GCM", *Climate Dynamics*, Vol. 45/11-12, pp. 3299-3316, http://dx.doi.org/10.1007/s00382-015-2540-2. [29]

Kim, J. et al. (2020), "Extensive fires in southeastern Siberian permafrost linked to preceding Arctic Oscillation", *Science Advances*, Vol. 6/2, p. eaax3308, http://dx.doi.org/10.1126/sciadv.aax3308. [24]

Lanphear, B. (ed.) (2015), "Association between Traffic-Related Air Pollution in Schools and Cognitive Development in Primary School Children: A Prospective Cohort Study", *PLOS Medicine*, Vol. 12/3, p. e1001792, http://dx.doi.org/10.1371/journal.pmed.1001792. [3]

Lanzi, E. and A. Dellink (2019), *Economic interactions between climate change and outdoor air pollution*, OECD Environment Working Papers, No. 148, OECD Publishing, Paris, https://doi.org/10.1787/8e4278a2-en. [32]

Ma, J., H. Hung and R. Macdonald (2016), "The influence of global climate change on the environmental fate of persistent organic pollutants: A review with emphasis on the Northern Hemisphere and the Arctic as a receptor", *Global and Planetary Change*, Vol. 146, pp. 89-108, http://dx.doi.org/10.1016/j.gloplacha.2016.09.011. [17]

Nieuwenhuijsen, M. et al. (2014), "Air pollution and human fertility rates", *Environment International*, Vol. 70, pp. 9-14, http://dx.doi.org/10.1016/j.envint.2014.05.005. [2]

O'Garra, T. (2017), "Economic value of ecosystem services, minerals and oil in a melting Arctic: A preliminary assessment", *Ecosystem Services*, Vol. 24, pp. 180-186, https://doi.org/10.1016/j.ecoser.2017.02.024. [16]

OECD (2020), *Non-exhaust Particulate Emissions from Road Transport: An Ignored Environmental Policy Challenge*, https://doi.org/10.1787/4a4dc6ca-en. [31]

OECD (2019), *Accelerating Climate Action: Refocusing Policies through a Well-being Lens*, OECD Publishing, Paris, https://dx.doi.org/10.1787/2f4c8c9a-en. [11]

OECD (2016), *The Economic Consequences of Outdoor Air Pollution*, OECD Publishing, Paris, https://dx.doi.org/10.1787/9789264257474-en. [1]

RCP (2016), *Every breath we take: the lifelong impact of air pollution | RCP London*, Report of a working party of the Royal College of Physicians. London., https://www.rcplondon.ac.uk/projects/outputs/every-breath-we-take-lifelong-impact-air-pollution (accessed on 30 November 2020). [10]

Science for Environment Policy (2017), "FUTURE BRIEF: Persistent organic pollutants: towards a POPs-free future Science for Environment Policy The contents and views included in Science for Environment Policy are based on independent research and do not necessarily reflect the position of the European Commission", *Future Brief 19. Brief produced for the European Commission DG Environment.*, http://dx.doi.org/10.2779/170269. [19]

Screpanti, A. and A. De Marco (2009), "Corrosion on cultural heritage buildings in Italy: A role for ozone?", *Environmental Pollution*, Vol. 157/5, pp. 1513-1520, http://dx.doi.org/10.1016/j.envpol.2008.09.046. [13]

UNEP (2010), *Protectic Arctic Biodiversity: limitation and strengths of environmental agreements*, https://wedocs.unep.org/handle/20.500.11822/7871 (accessed on 8 December 2020). [15]

Walton, H. et al. (2015), *Understanding the Health Impacts of Air Pollution in London For: Transport for London and the Greater London Authority*, Title: TFL 90419 Task 5: Understanding the Health Impacts of Air Pollution in London, https://www.london.gov.uk/sites/default/files/HIAinLondon_KingsReport_14072015_final_0.pdf (accessed on 30 November 2020). [9]

Wang, X. et al. (1997), "Association between air pollution and low birth weight: a community-based study.", *Environmental Health Perspectives*, Vol. 105/5, pp. 514-520, http://dx.doi.org/10.1289/ehp.97105514. [6]

WHO (2013), *Health risks of air pollution in Europe – HRAPIE project. Recommendations for concentration-response functions for cost-benefit analysis of particulate matter, ozone and nitrogen dioxide*, World Health Organization, Regional Office for Europe, Bonn, Germany, https://www.euro.who.int/en/health-topics/environment-and-health/air-quality/publications/2013/health-risks-of-air-pollution-in-europe-hrapie-project.-recommendations-for-concentrationresponse-functions-for-costbenefit-analysis-of-particulate-matter,-ozone-and-nitrogen-dioxide (accessed on 30 November 2020). [8]

Wu, X. et al. (2020), *Exposure to air pollution and COVID-19 mortality in the United States*, Cold Spring Harbor Laboratory, http://dx.doi.org/10.1101/2020.04.05.20054502. [12]

Yumashev, D. et al. (2019), "Climate policy implications of nonlinear decline of Arctic land permafrost and other cryosphere elements", *Nature Communications*, Vol. 10/1, http://dx.doi.org/10.1038/s41467-019-09863-x. [27]

Zhang, X., X. Chen and X. Zhang (2018), "The impact of exposure to air pollution on cognitive performance", *Proceedings of the National Academy of Sciences*, Vol. 115/37, pp. 9193-9197, http://dx.doi.org/10.1073/pnas.1809474115. [7]

Annex A. ENV-Linkages model

Overview of the ENV-Linkages model

The OECD ENV-Linkages model is a dynamic multi-sectoral, multi-regional CGE model that links economic activities to energy and environmental issues. A more comprehensive model description is given in Chateau et al. (2014[1]). While ENV-Linkages can provide emission projections for greenhouse gases and air pollutants, for this report, emissions of air pollutants are provided by the GAINS model, based on ENV-Linkages' economic projections. Indeed, GAINS can provide a higher regional disaggregation with country-specific emission projections for all Arctic Council countries.

Production in ENV-Linkages is assumed to operate under cost minimisation with perfect markets and constant return to scale technology. The production technology is specified as nested constant elasticity of substitution (CES) production functions in a branching hierarchy. This structure is replicated for each output, while the parameterisation of the CES functions may differ across sectors. The nesting of the production function for the agricultural sectors is further re-arranged to reflect substitution between intensification (e.g. more fertiliser use) and extensification (more land use) of crop production, or between intensive and extensive livestock production. The structure of electricity production assumes that a representative electricity producer maximises its profit by using the different available technologies to generate electricity using a CES specification with a large degree of substitution. The structure of non-fossil electricity technologies is similar to that of other sectors, except for a top nest combining a sector-specific resource with a sub-nest of all other inputs. This specification acts as a capacity constraint on the supply of the electricity technologies.

Energy is a composite of fossil fuels and electricity. In turn, fossil fuel is a composite of coal and a bundle of the "other fossil fuels". At the lowest nest, the composite "other fossil fuels" commodity consists of crude oil, refined oil products and natural gas. The values of the substitution elasticities are chosen as to imply a higher degree of substitution among the other fuels than with electricity and coal.

The model adopts a putty/semi-putty technology specification, where substitution possibilities among factors are assumed higher with new vintage capital than with old vintage capital. In the short run, this ensures inertia in the economic system, with limited possibilities to substitute away from more expensive inputs. However, in the longer run, this implies relatively smooth adjustment of quantities to price changes. Capital accumulation is modelled as in the traditional Solow/Swan neo-classical growth model.

Household consumption demand is the result of static maximisation behaviour, which is formally implemented as an "extended linear expenditure system". A representative consumer in each region – who takes prices as given – optimally allocates disposal income among the full set of consumption commodities and savings. Savings are considered as a standard good in the utility function and do not rely on forward-looking behaviour by the consumer. The government in each region collects various taxes to finance government expenditures. Assuming fixed public savings (or deficits), the government budget is balanced through the adjustment of the income tax on consumer income. In each period, investment net-of-economic depreciation is equal to the sum of government savings, consumer savings and net capital flows from abroad.

International trade is based on a set of regional bilateral flows. The model adopts the Armington specification, assuming that domestic and imported products are not perfectly substitutable. Moreover, total imports are also imperfectly substitutable between regions of origin. Allocation of trade between partners then responds to relative prices at the equilibrium.

Market goods equilibria imply that, on the one side, the total production of any good or service is equal to the demand addressed to domestic producers plus exports; and, on the other side, the total demand is allocated between the demands (both final and intermediary) addressed to domestic producers and the import demand.

ENV-Linkages is fully homogeneous in prices and only relative prices matter. All prices are expressed relative to the numéraire of the price system that is arbitrarily chosen as the index of OECD manufacturing exports prices. Each region runs a current account balance, which is fixed in terms of the numéraire. One important implication from this assumption in the context of this report is that real exchange rates immediately adjust to restore current account balance when countries start exporting/importing emission permits.

As ENV-Linkages is a recursive-dynamic model and does not incorporate forward-looking behaviours, price-induced changes in innovation patterns are not represented in the model. However, the model does entail technological progress through an annual adjustment of the various productivity parameters in the model, including autonomous energy efficiency and labour productivity improvements. Furthermore, as production with new capital has a relatively large degree of flexibility in choice of inputs, existing technologies can diffuse to other firms. Thus, within the CGE framework, firms choose the least-cost combination of inputs, given the existing state of technology. The capital vintage structure also ensures that such flexibilities are larger in the long run than in the short run.

The sectoral and regional aggregation of the model, as used in the analysis for this report, are given in Tables A.1 and A.2, respectively.

Table A.1. Sectoral aggregation of ENV-Linkages

Agriculture	Manufacturing
Paddy rice	Paper and paper products
Wheat and meslin	Chemicals
Other grains	Non-metallic minerals
Vegetables and fruits	Metals n.e.s. (not elsewhere specified)
Sugar cane and sugar beet	Fabricated metal products
Oil seeds	Other manufacturing
Plant fibres	Motor vehicles
Other crops	Electronic equipment
Livestock	Textiles
Forestry	
Fisheries	
Natural resources and energy	**Services**
Coal	Land transport
Crude oil	Air transport
Gas extraction and distribution	Water transport
Other mining	Construction
Petroleum and coal products	Trade other services and dwellings
Electricity (5 technologies*)	Other services (government)

Note: Fossil fuel-based electricity: combustible renewable and waste-based electricity; nuclear electricity; hydro and geothermal; solar and wind.
Source: ENV-Linkages.

Table A.2. Regional aggregation of ENV-Linkages

Macro regions	ENV-Linkages countries and regions
OECD America	Canada
	Chile
	Mexico
	United States
OECD Europe	EU large 4 (France, Germany, Italy, United Kingdom)
	Other OECD EU (other OECD EU countries)
	Other OECD (Iceland, Norway, Switzerland, Turkey, Israel)
OECD Pacific	Oceania (Australia, New Zealand)
	Japan
	Korea
Rest of Europe and Asia	China
	Non-OECD EU (non-OECD EU countries)
	Russia
	Caspian region
	Other Europe (non-OECD, non-EU European countries)
Latin America	Other Latin-American countries
Middle East & North Africa	Middle-East
	North Africa
South and South-East Asia	India
	Indonesia
	ASEAN9 (other ASEAN countries)
	Other Asia (other developing Asian countries)
Sub-Saharan Africa	Other Africa (other African countries)

Source: ENV-Linkages.

The baseline economic trends are described in the recent *Global Material Resources Outlook to 2060* (OECD, 2019[2]). For the dynamic calibration of ENV-Linkages to 2050, macroeconomic projections are based on two long-run macroeconomic growth models. First, the growth scenarios result from simulations of the OECD Economics Department (Guillemette and Turner, 2018[3]). These projections cover 42 OECD and G20 countries up to 2060. Second, the ENV-Growth model, hosted at the OECD Environment Directorate, is used to complete these projections for countries not covered by the OECD's Economic Department. Together, macroeconomic projections are provided for almost 180 countries.

The baseline construction also reproduces specific sectoral trends for the energy and agricultural sectors. Energy system projections are calibrated to the *2018 World Energy Outlook* (IEA, 2018[4]) and they are fundamental to ensure that energy-related emissions reflect the latest energy trends.

Modelling the economic feedbacks of air pollution in ENV-Linkages

The economic feedbacks of air pollution are modelled directly in ENV-Linkages following a production function approach, as outlined in *The Economic Consequence of Outdoor Air Pollution* (OECD, 2016[5]). This means that market impacts directly affect specific elements in the economic system, such as labour productivity or land productivity. The impacts are thus modelled as changes in the most relevant parameters of the production function underlying the model structure.

Changes in *health expenditures* are implemented in the model as a change in demand for health services (in the model part of the aggregate non-commercial services sector). These health expenditures reflect costs related to treatments of the illnesses as well as hospital admissions. The additional health expenditures affect both households and government expenditures on healthcare. The distinction between households and government expenditures is based on World Bank data on the proportion of healthcare expenditures paid by households and by the government (World Bank, 2015[6]). Health expenditures caused by outdoor air pollution are calculated multiplying the number of cases for each illness (e.g. chronic bronchitis) with a corresponding unit cost value (e.g. the health expenditures linked to a case of chronic bronchitis), using a methodology similar to the cost of illness approach in which only the tangible healthcare costs are considered. The reference unit values for the healthcare costs used in this report for the OECD, which are outlined in Table A.3, are established based on existing studies, as elaborated in Holland (2014[7]). These representative OECD values are then adapted to individual countries, multiplying them by the ratio of each country's income and the average OECD income, for each year.

Table A.3. Unit values used to calculate healthcare costs

USD, 2017 PPP exchange rates

Effect	Value
Chronic bronchitis in adults	15,810
Bronchitis in children	69
Equivalent hospital admissions (respiratory and cardiovascular diseases)	4,149

Note: Values are for the OECD. They are unit values and as such, they refer to costs per statistical life, cases of illness, hospital admissions and days with restricted activity.
Source: Own evaluation based on Holland (2014[7]).

Changes in *labour productivity* are directly implemented in the model as percentage changes in the regional productivity of the labour force. Productivity losses are calculated from lost work days, following the methodology used in Vrontisi et al. (2016[8]). This methodology calculates labour productivity losses as proportional to the number of lost work days, as compared to the average number of work days per year in each region (World Bank, 2014[9]).

Changes in *crop yields* are implemented in the model as a combination of changes in the productivity of the land resource in agricultural production, and changes in the total factor productivity of the agricultural sectors. This specification, which is in line with OECD (2015[10]), mimics the idea that agricultural impacts affect not only purely biophysical crop growth rates but also other factors such as management practices. Air pollution affects crop yields heterogeneously in different world regions, depending on the concentrations of ground-level ozone. Overall, the demand for agricultural products, which changes over time in the model even in the baseline scenario, is affected in each region by the air pollution-driven changes in crop yields.

Once the shocks from the air pollution impacts are incorporated in ENV-Linkages, the model finds a new equilibrium that takes into account the impacts of air pollution. Following the adjustment processes that takes place in the model, the direct impacts of air pollution also result in indirect impacts. For instance, an increased demand for healthcare may result in a lower demand for other services, while changes in crop yields for certain crops may result in changes in production of substitute crops or related economic activities (such as food production). These changes in production can then lead to changes in trade patterns.

Annex B. Methodology for calculating and valuing mortality and morbidity impacts

This annex provides a detailed overview of the methodology used to create projections of health impacts of air pollution, including both mortality and morbidity, as well as their valuation in monetary terms. The first part explains the methodology used to calculate air pollution-related deaths linked with high concentrations of fine particulate matter, while the second part focuses on morbidity impacts. Finally, the last part presents the methodology used for the monetary valuation of mortality and morbidity impacts.

Mortality calculations

Following the Global Burden of Disease (GBD, 2018[11]), the total amount of air pollution-related deaths attributable to outdoor air pollution corresponds to the sum of the deaths due to each disease for which there is an increased risk due to outdoor air pollution of fine particulate matter and ground-level ozone. For $PM_{2.5}$, these illnesses are: ischemic heart disease (IHD), strokes, chronic obstructive pulmonary disease (COPD), lung cancer (LC), lower respiratory infection (LRI) and diabetes mellitus type 2 (DM). For ground-level ozone, the Global Burden of Disease (GBD, 2018[11]) indicates that exposure to increases the risk of deaths due to chronic obstructive pulmonary disease (COPD).

The mortality calculations for each disease is based on this formula:

$$D_t^r = AF \cdot BD_r^t$$

$$with$$

$$AF = \left(1 - \frac{1}{RF}\right)$$

Where deaths related to air pollution (D) are derived as the product between baseline deaths (BD) for each disease and the attributable fraction (AF), namely the fraction of baseline mortalities that can be associated with air pollution. The attributable fraction (AF) is derived as ($1-1/RF$), where RF is a disease-specific risk factor, which reflects how, for each disease, the risk of dying because of air pollution increases with higher concentrations of pollutants ($PM_{2.5}$ and ground-level ozone).

The calculations of the health risks (RF) linked with exposure to $PM_{2.5}$ used in this report rely on the GBD's Integrated Exposure-Response (IER) functions (Cohen et al., 2018[12]; Burnett et al., 2014[13]). These functions are non-linear and become flat at higher exposures. The formula contains various parameters, one of which is the zero risk threshold, which is set at 2.5 µg/m³ concentrations of $PM_{2.5}$.

For ground-level ozone, the RF is based on the following formula:

$$RF = e^{\ln\left(\frac{RR}{10}\right)*(Conc-Conc\,thr)}$$

Where *Conc* is the concentration of ground-level ozone measure in part per billions (ppb), *Conc thr* is the zero risk threshold of ozone concentration and RR is the Relative Risk associated to ground-level ozone.

Following GBD (2018[11]), this study uses the seasonal average of daily maximum eight hours mean as the metric for ground-level ozone, the concentration threshold is flat at 29.1 ppm and at a relative risk of 1.06.

Baseline mortalities are obtained from the GBD results tool (GBD, 2018[11]). To create the projection for 2020-40 we use GBD foresight, which relies on GBD 2016 data (Institute for Health Metrics and Evaluation (IHME), 2018[14]). To avoid discontinuities between GBD 2016 foresight and GBD 2017 data after 2017, the foresight data were scaled with their respective GBD 2016 value in 2017; this correction factor was applied on all years beyond 2017. Therefore, the final foresight data in the current set differ slightly from the GBD 2016 foresight data because they were tuned to match the 2017 data from GBD 2017. For 2050, base mortalities are assumed equal to 2040 levels.

Morbidity impacts calculations

The morbidity impacts of $PM_{2.5}$ exposure that are quantified in this report are: the effect of chronic exposure on adult and childhood bronchitis, the effect of acute exposure on hospital admissions for respiratory and cardiovascular illness, restricted activity days, lost working days and asthma symptom days for children. The morbidity impacts for ground-level ozone are: the effect of acute exposure on hospital admissions for respiratory and cardiovascular illness and minor restricted activity days.

Quantifying morbidity effects requires detailed data, including the concentration response relationship, the size of population risk, and the prevalence of morbidity. However, this level of information is only available for a small number of countries. To obtain estimates at the global level, the morbidity impacts are extrapolated as a multiplier on mortality from air pollution exposure, based on the EU Clean Air Policy Package studies (Holland, 2014[7]; European Commission, 2013[15]). The advantage of assuming a linear relation between mortality and morbidity is that the calculation of morbidity automatically factors in the non-linearity in response functions that is accounted for in the mortality calculations. The drawback is that non-linearities are missed and that this approach cannot fully capture the connection between exposure to air pollution and illness.

The mortality-to-morbidity ratios are taken from the European Commission's Clean Air Policy Package studies (Holland, 2014[7]; European Commission, 2013[15]). The study by Holland (2014[7]) supplies region-specific morbidity-to-mortality ratios for the 28 European countries in which the package was implemented. To calculate morbidity impacts at the global level, for countries not covered by the Clean Air Policy Package studies, the average of the ratios of the European countries is used. While this extrapolation is not ideal, no data are available at the global level. This assumption is limiting, as it assumes that mortality-to-morbidity ratios throughout the world are similar to those of European countries. Furthermore, it implicitly assumes that healthcare provision is similar in all countries. For hospital admissions, it implies that European admission rates are typical of all other countries, when there is substantial variation around the world with respect to access to healthcare systems. This problem is particularly serious for developing countries, where access to healthcare is much lower. A similar issue arises with respect to lost working days. The European results are based on European rates of absenteeism, reflecting specific social welfare and employment conditions.

There are other limitations of the methodology used to calculate morbidity impacts in this report. Ideally, changes in behaviour (e.g. in diet, smoking habits, etc.), social changes (e.g. healthcare and employment) and medical changes (e.g. changes in healthcare systems and in treatment of diseases) over time and in different world regions should be explicitly factored into the analysis, but this is not possible owing to lack of data at the global level.

Valuation of the welfare costs of mortality and morbidity impacts

The valuation of the welfare costs of the health impacts of outdoor air pollution includes both mortality and morbidity. The total welfare costs are calculated by multiplying each impact considered (e.g. number of hospital admissions, cases of illness, and mortality) by estimates of the unit welfare cost of each impact (e.g. the welfare cost of a hospital admission, a case of illness, and a mortality).

Welfare costs of mortality

The welfare costs of air pollution-related mortality are obtained from a meta-analysis of a large number of studies of individuals' willingness to pay (WTP) for a marginal reduction in their risk of mortality over time. Aggregating the individual results of the various WTPs in the meta-analysis allows us to quantify the so-called Value of a Statistical Life (VSL), a long-established metric that attributes a monetary value to life and, as a consequence, can be used to estimate the welfare costs of mortality (OECD, 2014[16]; OECD, 2012[17]). As a result of this meta-analysis, the base VSL in OECD countries is USD 3 million (2005 PPP) per life lost in 2005.

As this report has global coverage, it was necessary to calculate VSL values for countries outside the OECD. This report relies on the OECD database "Mortality and welfare cost from exposure to environmental risks" (OECD, 2020[18]) for the base year value for each region of the study, since it provides country-specific VSL for OECD countries and emerging economies. Welfare costs in this database are calculated using a methodology adapted from Roy and Braathen (2017[19]).

Furthermore, since the report also considers economic projections, the VSL values need to be adapted over time. A previous OECD study (OECD, 2014[16]) provides a benefit transfer methodology to determine country-specific VSL values from an OECD reference value, based on country income differentials. The benefit transfer methodology is used to adapt VSL to individual countries, but also to estimate its growth over time, as income rises. As argued in OECD (2006[20]), income should be used as the reference variable to adapt WTP over time, so as to avoid situations in which the WTP to save a statistical life rises faster over time than the rate of inflation. Existing studies – such as Costa and Kahn (2004[21]), who calculate the VSL changes in the United States for the period 1940-80 – find that VSL rises over time as income rises. The country-specific income levels over time that are necessary for the calculations are obtained from the International Monetary Fund until 2017 (IMF, 2019[22]) and from the economic projections of the OECD's ENV-Growth model, which are also used for the calibration of the ENV-Linkages model.

The formula used to calculate the VSL is:

$$VSL_r^t = VSL_{OECD}^{2017} \left(\frac{Y_r^t}{Y_{OECD}^t} \right)^\beta$$

Where Y is the average income (GDP per capita) of country r in year t expressed in 2017 USD PPP; and β is the income elasticity of VSL. The income elasticity measures the percentage increase in VSL for a percentage increase in income.

The income elasticity used to calculate the country-specific VSL values is a key parameter; choosing different values can alter the results for welfare costs. The income elasticity variable assumes that as incomes rise, the WTP for a marginal reduction in the risk of death also rises, but not quite in proportion to the rise in incomes. The meta-analysis (OECD, 2012[17]) finds that the income elasticity is in the range of 0.7-0.9 for OECD countries, with significantly higher income elasticities for countries in the bottom 40th percentile of income. However the range proposed in OECD (OECD, 2012[17]) was considered to be too low for low-income countries as using such values would imply unrealistically high WTP values for these countries. Existing work on VSL (Hammitt and Robinson, 2011[23]; Roy and Braathen, 2017[19]) supports the assumption that the impact of income elasticity on the WTP does not necessarily hold true for emerging economies. Thus, following previous OECD work (OECD, 2016[5]) this report differentiates elasticity values by income group and uses a slightly higher elasticity for low-income countries. Specifically the income elasticities used are: 0.8 for high-income countries, 0.9 for middle-income countries and 1 for low-income countries (where country groups are distinguished using the World Bank income thresholds).

Given the difficulty in establishing the WTP to reduce the risks of mortality and the high dependency of the results on the key parameter value of income elasticity, the welfare costs results need to be interpreted in the context of the uncertainty surrounding the VSL values. An uncertainty analysis on the parameter values is provided in (OECD, 2016[5]).

While the VLS values are surrounded by uncertainty, a change in methodology would not affect the overall policy results of the analysis, which show high welfare costs associated with the deaths caused by outdoor air pollution.

Welfare costs of morbidity

The analysis of the health impacts of air pollution in this report distinguishes between two types of costs related to illness, as outlined in OECD (2016[5]):

1. The healthcare costs that are used to calculate healthcare expenditures as input to calculate the macroeconomic consequences of air pollution (see Annex A). Healthcare costs reflect the expenditures linked with each case of illness (e.g. the costs of hospital admissions, of going to the doctors or of buying medicines).

2. Welfare costs of morbidity, which reflect the pain and suffering of each case of illness. In other words, welfare costs of morbidity reflect the disutility of illness.

The welfare costs of morbidity used here rely on previous work by the European Commission (Holland, 2014[7]), which provides unit values for the welfare costs of the morbidity impacts (Table B.1). Morbidity welfare costs are adjusted to specific countries based on income, using the benefit transfer methodology used for mortality. Although there is a bias in transferring estimates of the disutility of morbidity from existing studies, mostly developed in Europe, to the global context, the benefit transfer method is the only available technique in this context, since valuation studies on the welfare impacts of air pollution-related illnesses only exist for a few areas in the world.

Table B.1. Unit values used for analysing the welfare costs of morbidity

USD, 2017 PPP exchange rates

Effect	Value
Chronic bronchitis in adults (new cases)	74 526
Bronchitis in children (cases)	817
Equivalent hospital admissions (respiratory and cardiovascular diseases)	695
Restricted activity days	180
Minor restricted activity days (asthma symptom days)	58

Note: Values are for the OECD. They are unit values and as such they refer to costs per case of illness, hospital admissions and days with restricted activity.
Source: Own evaluation based on Holland (2014[7]).

References

Burnett, R. et al. (2014), "An Integrated Risk Function for Estimating the Global Burden of Disease Attributable to Ambient Fine Particulate Matter Exposure", *Environmental Health Perspectives*, Vol. 122/4, pp. 397-403, http://dx.doi.org/10.1289/ehp.1307049. [13]

Chateau, J., R. Dellink and E. Lanzi (2014), "An Overview of the OECD ENV-Linkages Model: Version 3", *OECD Environment Working Papers*, No. 65, OECD Publishing, Paris, https://dx.doi.org/10.1787/5jz2qck2b2vd-en. [1]

Cohen, A. et al. (2018), "Global estimates of mortality associated with long-term exposure to outdoor fine particulate matter", *Proceedings of the National Academy of Sciences*, Vol. 115/38, pp. 9592-9597, http://dx.doi.org/10.1073/pnas.1803222115. [12]

Costa, D. and M. Kahn (2004), "Changes in the Value of Life, 1940–1980", *Journal of Risk and Uncertainty*, Vol. 29/2, pp. 159-180, http://dx.doi.org/10.1023/b:risk.0000038942.18349.88. [21]

European Commission (2013), *The Clean Air Policy Package*, pp. No. SWD(2013)531, European Commission, Brussels, http://ec.europa.eu/governance/impact/ia_carried_out/docs/ia_2013/swd_2013_0531_en.pdf. [15]

GBD (2018), "Global Burden of Disease Study 2017: All cause Mortality and Life Expectancy 1950-2017, Global Burden of Disease Collaborative Network.", *Seattle, United States: Institute for Health Metrics and Evaluation (IHME)*. [11]

Guillemette, Y. and D. Turner (2018), "The Long View: Scenarios for the World Economy to 2060", *OECD Economic Policy Papers*, No. 22, OECD Publishing, Paris, https://dx.doi.org/10.1787/b4f4e03e-en. [3]

Hammitt, J. and L. Robinson (2011), "The Income Elasticity of the Value per Statistical Life: Transferring Estimates between High and Low Income Populations", *Journal of Benefit-Cost Analysis*, Vol. 2/1, pp. 1-29, http://dx.doi.org/10.2202/2152-2812.1009. [23]

Holland, M. (2014), *Cost-benefit Analysis of Final Policy Scenarios for the EU Clean Air Package*, Corresponding to IIASA TSAP Report No. 11, International Institute for Applied Systems Analysis (IIASA), Laxenburg, http://ec.europa.eu/environment/air/pdf/TSAP%20CBA.pdf (accessed on 9 March 2021). [7]

IEA (2018), *World Energy Outlook 2018*, International Energy Agency, Paris, https://dx.doi.org/10.1787/weo-2018-en. [4]

IMF (2019), *World Economic Outlook Database*, International Monetary Fund, https://www.imf.org/external/pubs/ft/weo/2019/02/weodata/index.aspx. [22]

Institute for Health Metrics and Evaluation (IHME) (2018), "Global Life Expectancy, All-Cause Mortality, and Cause-Specific Mortality Forecasts 2016-2040.", *Seattle, United States: Institute for Health Metrics and Evaluation (IHME).*, https://vizhub.healthdata.org/gbd-foresight/ (accessed on 2 December 19). [14]

Klimont, Z. et al. (forthcoming), "Global scenarios of anthropogenic emissions of air pollutants: ECLIPSE". [24]

OECD (2020), *Air quality and health: Mortality and welfare cost from exposure to air pollution (database)*, Statistics, OECD Environment, https://doi.org/10.1787/c14fb169-en (accessed on 3 November 2020). [18]

OECD (2019), *Global Material Resources Outlook to 2060: Economic Drivers and Environmental Consequences*, OECD Publishing, Paris, https://dx.doi.org/10.1787/9789264307452-en. [2]

OECD (2016), *The Economic Consequences of Outdoor Air Pollution*, OECD Publishing, Paris, https://dx.doi.org/10.1787/9789264257474-en. [5]

OECD (2015), *The Economic Consequences of Climate Change*, OECD Publishing, Paris, https://dx.doi.org/10.1787/9789264235410-en. [10]

OECD (2014), *The Cost of Air Pollution: Health Impacts of Road Transport*, OECD Publishing, Paris, https://dx.doi.org/10.1787/9789264210448-en. [16]

OECD (2012), *Mortality Risk Valuation in Environment, Health and Transport Policies*, OECD Publishing, Paris, https://dx.doi.org/10.1787/9789264130807-en. [17]

OECD (2006), *Cost-Benefit Analysis and the Environment: Recent Developments*, OECD Publishing, Paris, https://dx.doi.org/10.1787/9789264010055-en. [20]

Roy, R. and N. Braathen (2017), "The Rising Cost of Ambient Air Pollution Thus Far in the 21st Century: Results from the BRIICS and the OECD Countries", *OECD Environment Working Papers*, No. 124, OECD Publishing, Paris, https://doi.org/10.1787/19970900 (accessed on 26 April 2019). [19]

Vrontisi, Z. et al. (2016), "Economic impacts of EU clean air policies assessed in a CGE framework", *Environmental Science & Policy*, Vol. 55, pp. 54-64, http://dx.doi.org/10.1016/j.envsci.2015.07.004. [8]

World Bank (2015), *World Development Indicators*, Washington, DC., https://data.worldbank.org/indicator. [6]

World Bank (2014), *Doing Business 2015: Going Beyond Efficiency*, The World Bank, http://dx.doi.org/10.1596/978-1-4648-0351-2. [9]